MW00962829

GOVERNING ASIA

Reflections on a Research Journey

These thirty-eight essays by the professors and research fellows of the Lee Kuan Yew School of Public Policy is dedicated to the tenth anniversary of the School. The core theme of the essays is governance in Asia and what its governments and peoples are doing for the public good. As Asia rises, its policymakers and citizens, and indeed the rest of the world, are increasingly asking how this dynamic region is making public policy, what we can learn from that exciting, often turbulent process, and how Asians can do better. The School's diverse and international group of scholars have written a set of informal, provocative, and passionate essays about governance in Asia — its past, present, and future — and why they study it. The volume — a candid, engaging act of transparency and disclosure — is also an invitation to join the conversation on the problems and promise of Asia and the larger dialogue on public policy and policy research in a globalized world.

GOVERNING
ASIA

Reflections on a Research Journey

**The Lee Kuan Yew School of Public Policy
NUS, Singapore**

 **World Scientific**

NEW JERSEY · LONDON · SINGAPORE · BEIJING · SHANGHAI · HONG KONG · TAIPEI · CHENNAI

Published by

World Scientific Publishing Co. Pte. Ltd.

5 Toh Tuck Link, Singapore 596224

USA office: 27 Warren Street, Suite 401-402, Hackensack, NJ 07601

UK office: 57 Shelton Street, Covent Garden, London WC2H 9HE

Library of Congress Cataloging-in-Publication Data
Governing Asia : reflections on a research journey / by Lee Kuan Yew School of Public Policy, NUS, Singapore.
    pages cm
  Includes bibliographical references.
  ISBN 978-9814635073 (hardcover ; alk. paper) -- ISBN 978-9814635189 (softcover ; alk. paper)
  ISBN 978-9814635394 (ebook)
  1. Public administration--Asia. 2. Public administration--Study and teaching. I. Aoki, Naomi.
In search of good public administration and governance Container of (work): II. Lee Kuan Yew
School of Public Policy.
  JQ24.G7 2015
  351.5--dc23
                                                                            2014034480

British Library Cataloguing-in-Publication Data
A catalogue record for this book is available from the British Library.

Copyright © 2015 by World Scientific Publishing Co. Pte. Ltd.

All rights reserved. This book, or parts thereof, may not be reproduced in any form or by any means, electronic or mechanical, including photocopying, recording or any information storage and retrieval system now known or to be invented, without written permission from the publisher.

For photocopying of material in this volume, please pay a copying fee through the Copyright Clearance Center, Inc., 222 Rosewood Drive, Danvers, MA 01923, USA. In this case permission to photocopy is not required from the publisher.

In-house Editor: Juliet Lee Ley Chin

Typeset by Stallion Press
Email: enquiries@stallionpress.com

Printed in Singapore

Preface

The Lee Kuan Yew School of Public Policy (LKY School) is embarked on a noble mission: to educate the next generation of policymakers who will return to their homelands to improve the livelihoods of their fellow citizens and, in the process, transform Asia. Delivering world-class Masters and PhD programmes is the core business of the School. And we excel in what we do because we have a strong and dedicated team of faculty members and research fellows who are passionately committed to their work.

The passion that my colleagues bring to their teaching is one way in which they help the School fulfil its noble mission. Equally importantly, the passion that faculty and fellows bring to research is contributing significantly to the transformation of Asia. One little-known fact about the LKY School is that we have, in relative terms, one of the most diverse research communities of any School of Public Policy. We have over forty fulltime faculty and fellows, and they come from over ten countries. They come from large Asian economies like China, India, Japan, and South Korea, and from ASEAN countries like Indonesia, Malaysia, Philippines, Thailand, Singapore, and Vietnam. We also have colleagues from Australia, Canada, the Netherlands, Sri Lanka, and the USA.

This diversity is an enormous asset, as my colleagues are able to study, absorb, and write about many different national perspectives. The daily cross-fertilization of ideas and perspectives generates a unique research-active environment which is a true asset of the LKY School. As we reflected on what we could do to showcase the achievements of the School on its 10th anniversary, we struck upon the unusual idea that we should encourage the faculty and fellows to write about their research passions.

Researchers are notoriously independent. When the Vice Dean of Research, Kanti Bajpai, and I asked our colleagues to contribute essays on their research passions, and write them at short notice, we were uncertain how they would respond. We were therefore truly delighted when we received this collection of engaging and wide-ranging essays.

As a result of their enthusiastic response, at our 10th anniversary we have been able to produce a book that reflects on our research preoccupations and our inspirations. What are our research passions? Why are we interested in the subjects that we write about? What is important about those subjects? What lies ahead in our research programmes? An anniversary is a moment of celebration, but it is also a moment for reflection, taking stock of the journey travelled and the road in front. Immodestly, we think that the School has something to say about governance in Asia and how to improve it. Sharing our thoughts on governance in this indirect way might be instructive for others who are thinking about the prospects of Asia.

Collectively, these essays define the research journey of the School. We are happy to share the thirty-eight essays with you. They differ in length, in writing style and tone, in approach. Some are pithy and succinct; others are more discursive and meandering; some are very business-like and declarative, stating what they do and why quite baldly; others are more personal and musing and roll the wine of research around their tongues. All of them have interesting things to say about what is important in thinking about Asia's governance, whether it is from the point of view of public management and finance, international trade and investment flows, the management of natural resources and the environment, or national security and foreign policy.

I will not attempt to summarize the essays. There are thirty-eight of them, and this introduction would become a summary list rather than an invitation to the volume. Each essay deserves to be read in its own right and not be boiled down to a descriptive paragraph. Clearly, though, the essays range over at least six areas of research endeavour: development policy; regional and international economics; public management; social policy; resource management (energy, environment, water); and international security and global governance.

All of us at the School study Asia and its governance, principally from these six vantage points. We ask: How has Asia developed and what is the future of government-led development? How is Asia growing economically, what are the drivers of growth, and what is the place of regional and global trade and investment? Is growth equitably distributed or not? How does Asia deal with key areas of social policy such as health, pensions, and social security? What are the contours of urban policy in Asia and how will, or should, Asia deal with its steadily burgeoning move to the cities? As Asia develops, what are the implications for resources? How can societies access limited resources such as energy and water in particular? What to do about the rapidly-increasing environmental challenges of the continent? Will Asia be peaceful and cooperative and will it work within existing global norms, or will it shape global norms to suit its rise? Our essays will give readers an idea of how the faculty and research fellows at the School answer these questions.

In their research, my colleagues work with all kinds of different methodologies and conceptual and theoretical approaches. We value this ecumenical and pluralistic academic environment. Few, if any, of us are tied to a methodology and approach. Instead, we search for answers and allow ourselves to use whichever methods and approaches suit the problem at hand. I think the essays show this clearly enough. Some use quantitative methods and more formal models of inquiry. Others resort to qualitative methods and are more inductive and interpretive. Some are interested in testing general propositions and in articulating frameworks that might guide policy analysis; others use general propositions as a way of analysing specific policy challenges in particular instances and are more oriented to immediate problem solving. I think that a school of public policy should be marked by diversity of intellectual effort, that it should resist a monoculture, and that a hundred flowers should bloom.

Almost all academic research, whether in the natural or social sciences or even the humanities, is about how to make the world a better place for human beings. Schools of public policy focus above all on what governments can do in that quest. Governments are not the only agents that improve human existence, but the great discovery of the modern world, perhaps even greater than the discoveries of science, is that "The State" is a very powerful and potentially emancipatory institution that can make life more fulfilling for everyone. The economic crisis of 2008 has underlined the critical role of the state and, reading across the essays, I would hazard that we at the School consider governments to be vital in improving the public weal.

I have enjoyed learning more about what my colleagues do in their research. I hope you will too. The School embarks on its second decade of teaching and research with energy and enthusiasm and a sober sense of its mission. Asia will see the establishment of many more schools of public policy, which is all to the good. The Lee Kuan Yew School of Public Policy has been an educational pioneer in Asia, and is dedicated to thought leadership on governance and public policy in the years to come. *Governing Asia: Reflections on a Research Journey* is intended to share our thoughts and to invite our readers to join us in the journey ahead.

Kishore Mahbubani
Dean, Lee Kuan Yew School of Public Policy
August 2014

Contents

1 In Search of Good Public Administration and Governance

Naomi AOKI

My research areas are public administration and governance. I am interested not so much in what a government actually implements — that is to say, public policy — but rather how government organizations are structured and managed and how they work with other stakeholders in the delivery of public services. Reforming public administration and governance include altering decision-making arrangements vis-à-vis decentralization, introducing new pay and incentive schemes for civil servants, restructuring government bureaucracies, and collaborating with the private sector and citizens to make important decisions regarding public services. Often, these reforms are institutional, and they take place behind the scenes. As a result, their importance may not be evident in political debates as much as in the implementation of public policies. What follows is a description of my specific research areas and why I choose to do what I do.

Paths to Developing My Research Interests

Prior to starting my academic career in 2011, I was engaged in projects related to fiscal decentralization in post-apartheid South Africa (in 1999, as a college intern), and later, public expenditure management in Southeast Asia (as a World Bank consultant). Engaging in the World Bank's Public Expenditure Tracking Survey in the education sector taught me a great deal. Visiting local treasuries and schools in a developing country, I witnessed the problems hampering the effective delivery of primary education, particularly the lack of accountability and weak financial management capacity on the part of public administrators. This first-hand experience reinforced my belief that strong public administration and governance are essential for states to prosper. Quite often, however, these institutional facets are not very visible to the public, and the real consequences of public administration and governance reforms seem to remain unrecognized. Accordingly, these reforms presented themselves as research topics that have preoccupied me for a long time.

By the time I sought to do a doctoral degree in public administration, I was eager to know whether the fiscal decentralization reforms popular among donor agencies would actually work to improve government performance in developing countries and even in developed countries. The Maxwell School in Syracuse, in the United States, turned out to be the best place to study this topic because it offered courses in two areas of specialization: (i) Public Finance, Budgeting and Financial Administration and (ii) Organization Theory and Public Management. My dissertation explored the efficiency effects of decentralization, along with a number of conditions important to these effects. While completing my dissertation, I learned that empirical research on public administration, and decentralization in particular, is still evolving, due to the difficulties associated with measuring administrative decentralization. This awareness stimulated my current research interests, as I will explain.

I left Syracuse in early 2011, at a time when the world was witnessing multiple governance challenges. In January, in Africa, an overwhelming majority of South Sudanese people voted in a referendum to claim their independence, while in Egypt a large crowd of angry protesters in Tahrir Square raised a united voice against the authoritarian regime. I recall, back then, aid agencies were seeking public administration specialists who could engage in public administration reforms or civil service training in anticipation of new regimes to come. Then, on March 11, the world was shocked by the sight of a massive tsunami hitting Japan's Tohoku region and by the subsequent meltdown at the Fukushima nuclear plant. These disasters (hereafter referred to as the 3.11 disasters) furnished a watershed opportunity for Japan to reassess its disaster governance and reinvent it to better prepare for future calamities. The events of early 2011 cemented my interest in public administration and governance issues in general and in research on disaster governance in particular.

Current Research Pathways

Coming to Singapore from the United States was an eye-opening experience in its own right. It compelled me to think about public administration in Asian contexts, particularly about how theories and concepts developed in the US fare in Asian states and governments, and how public administrations in Asia functioned even before these theories and concepts emerged. Combined with my professional and personal experiences, this new context shaped my research focus in the following three areas:

- Administrative decentralization
- Collaborative governance in disaster management
- Public administration and governance in Asia.

Let me elaborate on each of these.

Administrative Decentralization. My interest in administrative decentralization is longstanding and traces its origin back to my experience in South Africa. As noted earlier, during the doctorate I became aware that empirical studies on decentralization are still evolving, due in part to the difficulties associated with measuring administrative decentralization, whereas measures of fiscal and political decentralization are relatively advanced. My research work with Professor Larry Schroeder led to a journal article entitled "An Approach to Measuring Subnational Administrative Autonomy in Education," which was published in the *International Journal of Public Administration* in 2014. This article captures the degree to which administrative decisions are decentralized in the education sector across countries, and it illuminates dimensions of decentralization that are not captured in the measures of fiscal and political decentralization.

Collaborative Governance in Disaster Management. Originally from Japan, I have both a personal and professional drive to draw governance lessons from the 3.11 disasters. One notable phenomenon occurring in the wake of the 3.11 disasters was the extent of collaboration among Japanese municipalities to help disaster-affected municipalities in Tohoku. Because research on this topic is scant, the first stage of my research had to be exploratory in nature, producing a case study entitled "Wide-Area Collaboration in the Aftermath of the March 11 Disasters in Japan: Implications for Responsible Disaster Management," forthcoming in the journal, *International Review of Administrative Sciences.* This article suggests the importance of the functioning of "wide-area collaboration" in (1) manpower support to disaster-affected municipalities and (2) disaster-debris processing, as a factor affecting the recovery and reconstruction outcome.

I am currently at the second stage of this project. Inspired by the findings in the exploratory stage, the goal of this stage is to empirically investigate factors affecting local governments' decisions to collaborate in the aforementioned two areas. In the wake of the 3.11 disasters, some local governments offered help to disaster-affected municipalities, whereas others remained inactive, and collaboration was seen to work better between some municipalities than between others. The current stage of research involves producing datasets to quantitatively investigate the reasons for these variations. With this analysis, I hope to make policy recommendations on how to promote collaboration in the future and make it work. Academically, I hope to contribute to the scholarship in the area of disaster governance, where systematic quantitative studies remain rare.

More important, my communications with stakeholders in Tohoku have cemented my interest in this research field. The local government officials I met during my field visits this year were extremely responsive to requests for interviews, and they expressed how deeply thankful they felt for the help from other countries, including Singapore, in the wake of the disasters. They hoped that I would write in English about what had happened in Tohoku, so that governance lessons from their challenging experiences could be disseminated widely and so that the world remembers the Tohoku disasters. Their fervent wish, that the Tohoku experience be analysed and understood, has driven my work.

Public Administration and Governance in Asia. Coming to Singapore inspired me to produce publications on public administration in Asia. At first, I was greatly inspired by Singapore's civil service, which exhibits a great degree of managerial orientation vis-à-vis its commitment to performance management, meritocracy, and management-by-objectives. Often, these techniques and practices are classified under the umbrella term New Public Management (NPM), which arguably originated in the US, Australia, New Zealand, and the UK. Despite their origins, they are strikingly present in Singapore.

This propelled me to take advantage of international datasets on education to show empirically that these techniques and practices are, in fact, institutionalized on the ground in Singapore's education sector. My findings were published in a journal article entitled "Institutionalization of New Public Management: The Case of Singapore's Education System" in the journal, *Public Management Review* (2013). The Singapore study provoked my current research agenda: to empirically investigate whether NPM works differently across countries with different political and socio-economic contexts. It has also inspired me to compare public administration in Singapore and Japan.

Concluding Remarks

While my earlier professional experiences deeply influenced my thinking on the importance of public administration and governance for the prosperity of states and the welfare of their people, these initial experiences also stimulated my scholarly journey. I am grateful to be a part of the Lee Kuan Yew School of Public Policy in its hallmark year and hope to produce research that benefits Asia and beyond.

2 A Third Generation Theory of Collective Action

Eduardo ARARAL

The core of my research programme revolves around the theme of institutions for collective action. In essence, collective action is concerned with how individuals, firms, and states cooperate to achieve mutually beneficial outcomes. Cooperation, however, is problematic because of *social dilemmas* or situations in which private interests are in conflict with collective interests. These dilemmas can arise, among others, when parties have asymmetric interests, when they put short-term selfish interests over long-term collective good, when commitments are not credible, and when actors have to compete as well as cooperate with each other.

In my view, collective action is one of the most important and ubiquitous subjects in the social sciences with significant implications for a large number of public policy and governance issues, from local to global. Scholars throughout history — from Rousseau, Hobbes, J.S. Mill, Smith, Machiavelli, Madison, Kautilya, and Confucius, among others — have been preoccupied with the problem of collective action.

Today, a large number of scholars — economists, political scientists, evolutionary biologists, game theorists, social psychologists, legal theorists, sociologists, and many others — remain fascinated by the puzzle of collective action. Political scientists, for instance, have studied collective action in terms of political parties and the stability of coalitions; voting and elections; prisoner's dilemma; self-governance; and the formation and functioning of trade unions and mass movements such as protest, civil war, and revolution.

Collective action has also been studied in terms of economic stagnation, international cooperation, global governance, international security alliances, the evolution of institutions or long-distance trade as well as guilds in Western Europe, Dutch water boards, decentralization in forestry and irrigation, the study of common pool resources, the tragedy of the commons, the tragedy of the anti-commons, global environmental externalities, foreign aid, tax compliance, not in my backyard (NIMBY) and facility siting, the origins of the state, the adoption of agricultural technology, and in terms of trust and cooperation.

Indeed, collective action is one of the most cited subjects in the social sciences. For instance, Elinor Ostrom's *Governing the Commons* (1990) has been cited at least 13,700 times; Garett Hardin's "Tragedy of the Commons" (1968) 20,000 times; James Coleman's *Foundations of Social Theory* (1994) 17,000 times; Robert Axelrod's *The Evolution of Cooperation* (1984) 21,000 times; Robert Putnam's *Social Capital* (1995) 8,500 times; and Sidney Tarrow's *Social Movements* (1994) 5,500 times.

Equally important, collective action problems lie at the heart of many important contemporary issues in international relations, global governance, and public policy. These include, to name a few, the challenges of coordinating and regulating international banking and finance; the stability of the European fiscal compact and the challenges of forming a political union; the future of the US-led Trans Pacific Partnership; dealing with the perennial fire and haze problem involving Indonesia, Singapore, and Malaysia; the future of the WTO; and the prospects of cooperation among the emerging BRICS economies (Brazil, Russia, India and China, South Africa). Collective action is also central to the prospects of a post-Kyoto treaty on climate change as well as cooperation among state and non-state actors in tackling a host of global governance issues in health, energy, climate change, transnational river basins, food safety, transnational crimes, among many others.

The core of my research agenda seeks to understand how institutions can be better designed to deal with these collective action problems. It builds on the first and second-generation theories of collective action to eventually improve the diagnostic and prescriptive tools used by scholars, analysts, and policymakers in designing and reforming institutions for collective action.

First and Second Generation Literature

Despite its being ubiquitous, old, well cited, important and a puzzling subject, there is as yet no widely accepted general theory of how institutions matter to collective action. The large number of examples I have cited suggests a failure to generalize the nature of the problem fifty years since Mancur Olson's classic *The Logic of Collective Action* (1965), Hardin's collective action essay (1982), and two decades since Ostrom's (1990) *Governing the Commons*. The study of the role of institutions has yet to evolve into an interdisciplinary project that appropriately brings together politics, economics, sociology, law, and administration. In essence, the literature can be divided into the first and second-generation theories of collective action.

The first generation theories of collective action — associated with game theorists — have attempted to generalize the problem as a prisoner's dilemma and the tragedy of the commons (Hardin, 1982; Rapoport, 1965; for a summary of this literature, see Holzinger, 2003). These theories have been helpful in modeling the fundamental structure of a collective action problem i.e. when private interests are at odds with collective interests. However, they have been criticized for (1) their unrealistic assumptions — an ergodic world, single type of player, communication and norms do not matter, and (2) their inability to explain widespread cooperation — rendering them questionable as a general theory of collective action (for instance, Ostrom, 1998).

The second-generation behavioural theories of collective action — associated with Ostrom –argue that collective action is a function of generalized trust, reputation, and reciprocity. Compared to the first generation theories of collective action, Ostrom's model recognizes (1) that there are multiple types of players; (2) that beliefs and norms evolve and play an important role in the development of reciprocity; and (3) that face to face communication matters and individuals can make credible commitments without a sword or threat of violence. Unlike the first generation theories which predict pessimistic outcomes of collective action, Ostrom's model posits a more conditional prediction: levels of cooperation will vary with the level of trust, which in turn is a function of reputation and reciprocity, among other structural variables. As such, the goal in designing a governance mechanism is to signal the trustworthiness of parties in collective action.

Like any other theory, Ostrom's behavioural model has room for improvement. First, it is limited to small, personal transactions in local common pool settings (North, 1999). Ostrom's design principles for the governance of local commons have yet to be systematically extended to large-scale global commons. As such, it is a special, not a general case. Second, Ostrom's model suggests that trust is the main determinant of cooperation. However, the trust model breaks down when we observe many cases of cooperation in the absence of trust or even in the face of distrust. Furthermore, the term trust as widely used in the social science literature as a predictor of cooperation suffers from the problem of post-hoc rationalization (Williamson, 1999). Finally, Ostrom does not explicitly and generally model collective action as a form of exchange and therefore does not explicitly account for the transaction cost dimensions of cooperation.

My Research Agenda

My research aims to develop a more general, third generation contracting theory of collective action. Building on the first and second-generation theories, I propose a more general, third generation, contracting theory of collective action by bringing together the work of Ostrom, Ronald Coase, John Williamson, and Robert North.

As the term implies, the contracting theory of collective action uses transaction cost and contract theory as the theoretical core. In contrast, Ostrom's model builds on behavioural theory and social psychology while the first generation uses non-cooperative game theory as the theoretical core. In Ostrom's model, the unit of analysis is the action situation while in game theory it is the structure of the game. In my model, I use transactions as my unit of analysis. For Ostrom, collective action is a problem of trust and reciprocity while in the first generation models it is a problem of commitment as typified by the prisoner's dilemma. In contrast, in the third generation model, collective action is a problem of contracting. Ostrom's model predicts that collective action will vary by the ambient level of trust while the first generation model predicts a pessimistic outcome of cooperation. In contrast, my model predicts conditional cooperation which will vary by type of transaction. The aim of my research programme is to better understand these attributes of transactions, how they matter to collective action, and how governance institutions can be better designed to address these problems.

In non-cooperative game theory, the primary governance mechanism is to defect (not to cooperate) while in Ostrom's model, it is to signal one's reputation of trustworthiness. In my model, the primary governance mechanism is to minimize contracting cost or the cost of measuring and enforcing contractual commitments as well as the maintenance of on-going relations. Finally, the main limitation of non-cooperative game theory is its unrealistic assumption about complete information by the players and the assumption of a static as against an ergodic world. Such a model is unable to explain widespread cooperation or deviation from the rationality prediction. Ostrom's model on the other hand is limited to small, personal, non-calculative transactions. It cannot explain cooperation given distrust or lack of trust and does not explicitly consider contractual dimensions of cooperation. Furthermore, trust and reciprocity as key concepts suffer from post-hoc rationalization and are difficult to falsify.

I have so far published 20 articles on various dimensions of this third generation theory of collective action.

In a paper published in *World Development* (Araral, 2009), I examine the factors affecting collective action in the commons based on a survey of 1,950 irrigation associations. Common pool resources such as forests, watersheds, coastal areas, rangeland, wildlife, and irrigation are critical to the livelihoods of millions of impoverished households worldwide in developing countries. The commons are characterized by rivalry in consumption and difficulty in exclusion, attributes that creates incentives that can potentially lead to over consumption and under provision of the public good, a collective action problem. The tragedy of the commons represented the conventional view in much of the 1970s and 1980s.

In the 1990s, scholars attempted to debunk the tragedy of the commons metaphor. This literature has identified at least two-dozen variables affecting collective action in the commons. However, there remain unsettled debates in the literature because of five methodological problems: over reliance on small-n case studies, specification problems, selection, and measurement and interaction-effects problems. The main contribution of the *World Development* paper is to address these five methodological problems in the literature to provide a more robust conclusion on the factors affecting collective action in the commons.

In another paper published in the *Journal of Public Administration Research and Theory* (Araral, 2009), I examine how foreign aid affects the incentives of bureaucracies managing the commons in developing countries. A key assumption in the public choice literature is that the provision of services by the visible hand of the government is an incidental effect of the incentives and constraints of voters, politicians, and bureaucrats. This view was prominent in the 1970s-1980s but lost its prominence as a research programme due to the paucity of empirical work and its inaccessible, mathematical approach.

The main contribution of my 2009 paper is to show why the public choice research programme should be revived and given more attention especially in the context of developing countries in Asia where good governance remains a significant challenge. I illustrate this by providing game theoretic reasoning and evidence to support the hypotheses of public choice. This game has two players: an infrastructure bureaucracy managing the commons in a developing country and its budget sponsor, the foreign donor. The model is important because foreign aid plays an important role in many developing countries, but little is empirically known about how it affects incentives and behaviour in public bureaucracies.

My findings suggest that bureaucrats have strong incentives to ensure bureau-cratic survival while donors are motivated by the growth of their loan portfolio. Foreign aid can have deleterious effects on the incentives of bureaucracies in man-aging the commons in developing countries. These results are broadly consistent with the theoretical expectations of institutional rational choice and the public choice literature: under certain conditions, the provision of government services is indeed an incidental effect of the incentives and constraints of bureaucrats and their budget sponsor. This finding calls into question the Pigouvian and Weberian notions that bureaucrats are benevolent maximizers of social welfare.

In a third paper, published in *Geoforum* (2013), I sought to examine the effects of physical geography on institutional choice for water governance. Using three case studies and controlling for the effects of production system, time, and culture, this paper compared how institutional choice varies with physical geography and asks whether this variation is mediated through the production system. The study finds that, indeed, variations in physical geography are associated with institutional variations and that this variation is mediated through the production system. Physical geography presents risks and opportunities for a production system — for example, flooding and droughts — and actors devise institutions to mitigate these risks or take advantage of these opportunities to achieve their production functions.

These findings have several implications in terms of the current debates on geography and institutions in general and institutions governing the commons in particular. First, the mediated and conditional effects of geography on institutions put into question the generalizability of arguments about environmental determinism on the one hand and institutional triumphalism on the other. In this view, institutions matter in evolutionary economic geography for their conditioning rather than determining effect on firm (or household) behaviour and regional development.

Second, institutional choices evolve as a mechanism to mitigate risks or to take advantage of opportunities. Here, the idea of institutional Darwinism might be of relevance i.e. institutional choices in the commons are a function of, among others, geography induced selection pressures. In the cases studied in the *Geoforum* paper, the selection pressure stems from persistent cycles of flooding and drought, which poses significant risks to the production system (farming) in a region, which influences the choice of institutions and in turn affects the production system and geography. Finally, if indeed geography matters to institutional choice, then these findings partly answer Ostrom's puzzle on the diversity of institutions governing the commons worldwide.

In another paper published in *Environmental Science and Policy* (Araral, 2013), I provide a critical appreciation of the considerable legacies of Ostrom and Hardin to the literature on the commons. First, how valid is Ostrom's critique of Hardin's tragedy of the commons? Second, how generalizable are studies arguing for Ostrom's institutional design principles for long-lived commons? Finally, how justified is Ostrom's critique of privatization, markets, and the Leviathan solutions to the tragedy of the commons? Based on a reassessment of the evidence and reinterpretation of Ostrom's work supplemented by field work, my preliminary findings suggest that, first, her critique of Hardin is valid in the special case of small-scale, locally-governed commons while Hardin's approach seems justified for large-scale, national, regional, and global commons. Second, studies arguing for the generalizability of Ostrom's institutional design principles are flawed and more rigorous studies are needed. Finally, I argue that Ostrom is justified in her critique of the Leviathan solution to the tragedy of commons, but a rethinking is needed of her critique of private property rights and markets.

In another paper, published in *Policy Sciences* (2014), I unpack the black box of institutions using transaction cost and mechanism design analysis to show how regulations can be better designed in developing countries when institutions are weak, unaccountable, corrupted, or not credible. Under these conditions, I show that efficient regulatory design has to minimize transaction costs, particularly agency problems, by having incentive compatible (self-enforcing) mechanisms. I conclude with a second-generation research agenda on regulatory design with implications for environmental, food and drug safety, healthcare, and financial regulation in developing countries.

The variety of examples I have shown — which looks at geography, property rights, regulations, markets, bureaucracies, the commons, among others — serves to illustrate the depth and breadth of the research agenda on developing a third generation contracting theory of collective action. I am currently working on ten other papers to build this research agenda to support my claims that collective action is a theoretically interesting and practically important subject in the study of public policy and institutions.

3 Growing Importance and Increasing Complexity: Research in Public Financial Management in Asia

Mukul G. ASHER

My research agenda over a professional career spanning four decades has primarily focused on applied, policy-oriented issues in the field of public financial management. The geographical focus of my research has been Asia. The research has involved both individual country analysis and comparative perspectives covering sub-regions in Asia.

The evolution of my research interests may be categorized in three phases, which I discuss in turn.

Graduate Studies and Immediate Aftermath: The First Phase

I pursued graduate studies during the 1960s and early 1970s in the United States, after undergraduate studies in Mumbai University in India. This was the period when Economic History and the History of Economic Thought were still a part of graduate studies in Economics, especially in those Departments focused on applied, policy-oriented research. These courses provided a much wider and deeper perspective on how economics as a discipline developed over time, particularly the kind of questions which were considered important at a given historical time.

The study of economic history helped graduate students guard against linear and singular causation in the analysis of economic conditions and the position of a given country or a region. The emphasis in these courses was on the experiences and issues of the Western countries. But I chose term paper topics such as "The Idea of Economic Progress in Hinduism" and "Economic Management and Kautilya's *Arthashastra*" — the *Arthashastra* being an ancient Indian treatise on statecraft, economic policy, and military strategy, written in Sanskrit in the Fourth Century BCE — to gain an understanding of my civilizational roots, its strengths and limitations.

Exposure to Economic History and to the History of Economic Thought, as I said, helped in not taking a linear view of any country or region's economic trajectory. The importance of technology also became much more evident, an area of limited coverage in the economics literature at the time. The opportunity cost of taking these courses was that I spent relatively little time on advanced econometrics and specialized courses in survey methods and related areas.

Richard Musgrave, Harold Groves, James Buchanan, Gordon Tullock, and Walter Heller were among the leading academic public finance economists during the 1960s and the 1970s. The research in applied public economics from the Brookings Institution in Washington D.C, where Henry Aaron, Joseph Pechman, Richard Netzer, Richard Goode, Stanley Surrey and others also worked, informed my research. Their work impressed on me the importance of high quality policy-oriented applied research in public finance, with considerable emphasis given to institutional and design matters in public finance policies. I was also impressed by the various modes of communication they used including participation in media debates and in testimony to U.S. government committees that helped improve the quality of public debate and decision-making.

This phase had a lasting impact on my research agenda, as it defined the scope and geographical focus of my research, and taught me to eschew mechanical adherence to any particular school of economic thought or to any one economic model or research technique. It also impressed on me the need to obtain requisite research materials from diverse sources, and wherever possible, to consult primary sources. The habit of not taking published data or material at face value, but rather attempting to understand how the data were put together was also formed during this phase.

My PhD dissertation was on constructing a macroeconomic model designed to help estimate fiscal leverage (a concept in whose development Richard Musgrave played a key role) of various taxes and expenditures for India, for the time period 1951–52 to 1965–66, the period coinciding with India's first three five-year plans. The research involved studying budgetary debates in the Indian Parliament, many of which were in the Hindi language.

Shift in Professional Base from the United States to Singapore: The Second Phase

The second phase of my research coincided with the shift in professional base from the United States to Singapore during the mid-1970s. Globally, this was the decade of stagflation and the sharp rise in energy prices in 1973 and in 1979. The period also coincided with the period of remarkable economic growth and progress in Southern and in East Asia, the rise of China after its 1978 reforms, and India's ascent after its 1991 reforms.

In the mid-1970s, public finance research, particularly comparative research involving Asian sub-regions, such as the Association of South East Asian Nations (ASEAN) established in August 1967, was at an initial stage. As ASEAN's importance grew with the rapid economic growth in the member countries and the forging of global inter-linkages (from the initial five countries, ASEAN membership grew to include all ten Southeast Asian countries), the need for comparative research on public finance issues became more evident.

My research interests in the second phase were primarily focused on the comparative analysis of fiscal systems in the ASEAN countries. One of the earlier research publications during this phase was a book with Anne Booth titled *Indirect Taxes in ASEAN*, published by Singapore University Press in 1983. This was the first book-length treatment of sales, excise, and international trade taxes in the ASEAN countries in a comparative framework.

There were several tax reform initiatives in Southeast Asia during this phase. These included a major reform involving Income Tax, Value-Added-Tax, and Land and Buildings Tax in Indonesia in 1983; introduction of a Value Added Tax in the Philippines in 1988; and of a Goods and Services Tax in Singapore in 1994.

The reform initiatives in the region provided me with numerous opportunities for research and communications with policymakers.

One of the research questions which puzzled me during this phase was the following: If Southeast Asian countries had similar formal legal provisions in promoting domestic and foreign investment, why were some countries more effective in obtaining investments? Research on this question led to the publication of a book with S. C. Rolt, M. Ariff, and M. H. Khan, *Fiscal Incentives and Economic Management in Indonesia, Malaysia, and Singapore* (Singapore: Asia-Pacific Tax and Investment Centre, 1992).

The main finding emerging from this research was that fiscal and other incentives designed to promote investment are effective only when they are used as a signal to investors that public policies will focus on the requirements essential for the promoted activity to become viable. When such incentives are used as a substitute for factors, such as lack of infrastructure or skilled manpower, essential for viability, their effectiveness is very limited. Much of the subsequent research has broadly corroborated this finding.

The 1997 East Asian financial crisis, and its fiscal implications, and how regional and multilateral institutions dealt with the crisis provided valuable lessons in the conduct of public finance research. The importance of the concept of fiscal risk and contingent liabilities of the government in the affected countries became evident — a lesson re-learnt on a much wider scale during the 2008 global economic crisis.

In the later part of this phase, I edited a book with David Newman, and Thomas Snyder entitled *Public Policy in Asia: Implications for Business and Government* (Westport, CT: Greenwood Publishing, 2001) which focused on the challenges of policy studies in the Asian context. By this time, a network of public policy researchers on Asia was emerging, making it easier to obtain the participation of specialists in fiscal, income security, public management, and other areas.

Global Demographic and Urbanization Trends: The Third Phase

The rapid ageing of populations — reflected in projections by the United Nations that, by 2050, the Total Fertility Rate globally (the mean number of children born to an average woman during her lifetime, with 2.15 signifying stable population) would go below 2.15 for the first time in human history — and the urban population constituting a majority of the world's population for the first time in 2008 are two major trends contributing to the third phase in my research. The 2008 global economic crisis and its continuing aftermath have exacerbated the public financial management challenges arising from the two trends noted above.

My research during this phase initially focused on narrower financial and fiscal issues in managing ageing populations and in devising sustainable social protection programmes. But gradually the research focus has broadened to include new areas.

The first is the research on non-conventional methods to fund government expenditure, including social protection programmes. Using public assets more productively, improving procurement systems, emission trading and a carbon tax, and public-private-partnerships (PPPS) are some of the examples of raising resources through non-conventional methods. My research focuses on the requirements for using them more effectively. This in turn has led to viewing public financial management in a more integrated manner, and from the perspective of outcome or results obtained, rather than in merely financial terms. One consequence has been that accounting methods and budgeting systems reforms acquire much greater importance than was the case earlier.

It is evident that the above area has the potential to generate many interesting and relevant research questions. I am exploring some of them, particularly on ways to use state assets more productively and the use of PPPs in social and in infrastructure sectors. A narrower research area concerns developing municipal bond markets in India.

The second area concerns policy, programme, and organizational coherence between pension or retirement financing arrangements and health care. In high-income countries, combined expenditure on pensions, health care, elderly care, and related social expenditure are in the range of 20 to 25 percent of GDP. Traditionally, pension and health care are undertaken by separate ministries and government organizations. If coordination between them results in cost savings, that could generate substantial fiscal space for funding social expenditure.

A preliminary examination of this issue has been published as a working paper — A. S. Bali and M. G. Asher, *Coordinating Pension and Healthcare Policies: An*

Exploratory Study (Tokyo: ADBI Working Paper 374, August 2012). Further research by me and my collaborators will focus on country case studies (India will be the first case study) on the feasibility of such coordination and methods to achieve it.

The third area of research in this phase concerns designing the pay-out phase of an individual rather than social risk-pooling pension scheme. The current provisions require purchase of annuity from accumulated savings during the working years. But uncertainties in longevity trends, in part due to unanticipated medical advances, and absence of sufficient products to manage long-term risk of annuity providers, have resulted in relatively less developed annuity markets, including in Asia. Research on options for managing the pay-out phase, including designing phased withdrawal programmes for individuals, is another area of inquiry that I am pursuing.

The fourth area concerns focusing on reforming pension arrangements of groups which have so far received relatively little attention. These include civil servants and military personnel. Preliminary work has begun, but I hope to focus more intensively on this issue in the coming period.

The four areas I have described here will generate many interesting and challenging research questions. I therefore very much look forward to the third phase of my research agenda.

4 India on My Mind

Kanti BAJPAI

I've devoted most of my academic energies to studying my own country, particularly its external behaviour, and asking questions such as — How does India interact with its neighbours and the great powers? Is it as idiosyncratic and ad hoc as commentators have claimed? For a country that entered international society with a very public commitment to international peace and cooperation, it has a rather impressive record of conflict and violence. Why so? Can it overcome this rather melancholy history?

Why India? I suppose because (a) I'm Indian, (b) as a Foreign Service "brat", I was constantly arguing about India, and (c) its potential to do both harm and good is considerable and therefore worth understanding. India is personal: I wanted to live and raise a family in India, and thinking and writing about the country was (and is) never a merely academic choice. India is also exasperating. It so often does things that no one, not even Indians, quite understand. A perceptive foreign friend claims that she comes to India because it represents the most egregious and the most enlightened. Of the Soviet Union's foreign policy Winston Churchill said that it is "a puzzle inside a riddle wrapped in an enigma, and the key is Russian nationalism." My friend is on to something about India, and Churchill could have been referring just as easily to Indian foreign policy.

As a doctoral student, I had started out studying India's civil-military relations, grappling with the puzzle of why the Indian Army had stayed out of politics when the Pakistani and Bangladeshi armies, both brother armies, had repeatedly intervened. On the other hand, my graduate fellowship was funded by the international security programme at the University of Illinois, and this nudged me to study India's external behaviour instead. Gradually, therefore, my focus shifted.

Much of what was written about India's foreign policy at the time was focused on the country's conflicts, particularly with its neighbours. Normatively and academically, I was drawn to the possibilities of cooperation. As India's prospects were connected to the prospects of South Asia as a whole, I became interested in regional cooperation. Could New Delhi lead an effort at cooperation? The South Asian Association of Regional Cooperation (SAARC) had just been launched in 1980 and promised a new era for over a billion people — my dissertation attempted to explain why the seven South Asian countries had finally attempted to cooperate given their rather anemic history of collaboration.

After the dissertation, I continued to write about regionalism in South Asia and on military cooperation between India and Pakistan and India and China. At the end of the Cold War, there was a sense the world had survived the antagonism between the US and Soviet Union by investing in arms control, military stabilization measures, and tacit but also explicit agreements on the limits of geopolitical competition. With India and Pakistan on the brink of going nuclear, it seemed to me that arms control, confidence-building measures, and regional order-building in South Asia were vital things to think about.

As SAARC foundered, and as India and Pakistan slipped into a pattern of chronic, low-level conflict after the cold peace of the 1970s, my attention turned increasingly to South Asia's incipient nuclearization. By the late 1980s it was clear that India and Pakistan would go nuclear. Would this, as deterrence proponents argued, bring stability and peace; or would it, as critics argued, promote instability and conflict? I sided with the critics of deterrence. I'd co-authored a book on the confrontation between India and Pakistan in 1986–87 which occurred in the shadow of nuclear weapons, and my instinct was that nuclearization was dangerous. Rather controversially at the time, I wrote several articles against nuclear weapons, arguing that India could be secure without the bomb.

Then, in May 1998, India and Pakistan tested eleven nuclear devices between them and declared that they were *de facto* nuclear weapons states. I'd argued against India's decision to test, but I recognized that it was almost impossible for opponents of the bomb to turn back the clock. My thoughts therefore turned to the state of India's nuclear preparedness and the requirements of a stable deterrent. It was an uneasy position to be in: arguing against deterrence and, almost simultaneously, writing about the need to strengthen or stabilize India's deterrent. I didn't like nuclear weapons, but I had to accept that nuclear weapons were now part of Indian security policy; and, if so, a robust and stable deterrent posture was inescapable.

At the time, I was teaching at Jawaharlal Nehru University (JNU) and was sitting in dozens of seminars and conferences on nuclear policy. Listening to the debates in Delhi, I realized that India's nuclear proponents held to three distinct perspectives: two "minimalist" and one "maximalist". Using the writings of Indian security specialists, I attempted to disentangle the three perspectives and show that there existed differences on key policy choices. Fundamentally, I suggested, the rival perspectives were based on quite different views of deterrence. The question was: which deterrent posture was better for India?

This work led me to look more closely at the role of ideas in shaping policy. In 1992, George Tanham of the RAND Corporation had written a provocative monograph on Indian strategic culture, arguing in essence that the country didn't have much of a strategic culture. In 1997, I co-edited a volume that included two of Tanham's essays on India and several lively responses to him. With this book and building on my nuclear schools essay, I decided to look more closely at India's grand strategic ideas and the nature of India's international thought: Did Indians think grand strategically, and if so, what were their leading ideas? How had Indians conceived of international life, and did India have a tradition of international thought? These questions were often debated in my classes at JNU, where I defended the notion that Indians had thought quite extensively about both grand strategy and international politics. In a series of essays, I set about trying to show that this was indeed the case.

One way into the problem was offered by the discussion of "order and justice" in International Relations (IR). Hedley Bull, a leading member of the English School of IR, had argued that there was a deep tension between the imperatives of order and the demands for justice in international life. At about this time, Andrew Hurrell and Rosemary Foot at Oxford University along with John Lewis Gaddis of Ohio State University invited me to write an essay on India's conception of order and justice.

The essay argued that modern India had four schools of international thought, from which one could abstract conceptions of order and justice, namely, Nehruvianism, neo-liberalism, Gandhianism, and Hindu nationalism. The Nehruvian view had been dominant in India, but the other viewpoints were not without influence. The essay was not terribly successful in settling the debate between order and justice, but it gave me the opportunity to delve into Indian international thought and identify the most influential lines of thinking.

Tanham's essay reflected a widely held view to the effect that India had no grand strategy. If grand strategy is the combination of diplomatic, military, political, economic, and cultural resources deployed for national security, then the general view was that after Nehru the country had no larger plan or approach. Drawing once again on contemporary debates in India, I argued that there were three leading grand strategic schools of thought: Nehruvianism, neo-liberalism, and hyper-realism. I concluded that after the Cold War and in the wake of globalization the neo-liberals were dominant intellectually and that Indian policy was marked by neo-liberal preferences. At base, my aim was to showcase the richness of thought, to pitch the various schools against each other and, somewhat grandiosely, to provoke Indian security experts to be more alert to the intellectual roots of various lines of policy and to weigh the risks and dividends of strategic choices.

In describing India's grand strategic thought, I had placed internal security and relations with Pakistan, China, and the US at the centre of the contention between different schools. Not having written much on domestic politics, in 2002 I agreed to write a short, essayistic book for Penguin India called *Roots of Terrorism* which dealt with the causes of separatist violence and India's management of secessionist movements. With this, my academic writing tapered off, as I somewhat eccentrically took six years out of university life to be Headmaster of my old school.

By 2009, I had returned to the university and turned my attention to India's relations with China. With the Middle Kingdom's astonishing rise and the global economic crisis decimating Western economies, India's stance towards its great northern neighbour was becoming pivotal to its external policy. Indians were palpably envious of China's success and feared its growing power. Strategically, China appeared to be encircling India and, in some more fevered imaginations, preparing for war. A spate of books by Indian and Western authors suggested that the two giants of Asia were ineluctably pitted against each other. At the same time — reassuringly — New Delhi's policies towards Beijing were constructive and measured. The question was: would the Chinese and Indian governments hold to a sensible, moderate posture?

In 2011, I joined the LKY School and teamed up with Huang Jing to write about India-China relations. The book we are working on accepts that the relationship is marked by conflict, but it asks "Can the giants of Asia cooperate?" Virtually every body of international relations theory has a place for cooperation amidst conflict. This suggests that the answer must at least be a qualified yes. The book attempts to deal both with the older conflicts between the two countries — the unsettled border, China's relationship with Pakistan, interference in each other's domestic politics — and with potential future conflict in different regions of the world (principally in Asia) and over scarce resources (water, food, energy). It tries to show that the two have a history of cooperation and that they can cooperate in the future, on bilateral, regional, and global matters.

What lies ahead? The study of India of course, but perhaps more than just India… First, I want to return to Indian grand strategic thought and finish a full-length book on the subject. In the end, I want to show that the roots of grand strategic thinking are in political ontology and therefore ideology. Second, with Siddharth Mallavarapu of South Asia University, I am putting together an anthology of Indian international thought in the modern period, from the late 19th century to the late 20th century, and we hope to write a series of essays on how India has thought about international life. Third, I am keen to write a book on India in comparative context, arguing that despite the triumphalist accounts of the past two decades, the country confronts enormous development and governance challenges and that its administrative and political capacity to meet those challenges is woefully inadequate — in short, to dramatize the fact that India is at a dangerous cusp. Fourth, I see a huge arc of crisis stretching from North India to North Africa. This is arguably the most volatile area in the world, highly militarized, and obsessed with historical wrongs and hatreds, all of which make for a combustible future. The question is: what is fuelling the crisis? What might be the consequences of the various antagonisms? Can anything be done to lift the region out of its morass?

Obviously, this account of my research pathway presents a rather neat picture. In fact, it was all quite jumbled and jagged. It's worth saying too that while we do research to earn a living and to make a difference to the world, a good part of what drives us is sheer pleasure — of making nice patterns out of the messiness around us, of trying to say something no one else has said, and of being patted on the head. So in the end let me confess to the attractions of both opportunism and pleasure in research!

5 New Mindsets: Solving the World's Water and Wastewater Problems

Asit K. BISWAS

My interest in water developed in a circuitous way. When I decided to pursue an academic career, I joined the University of Strathclyde in Glasgow. I wanted to be a specialist in soil mechanics and foundation engineering. The tradition in Strathclyde at the time was that the newest hire had to teach the subject for which there was no lecturer available. Soil mechanics had more than its fair share of lecturers in those days, but hydraulics and fluid mechanics did not have many. I was thus forced to teach this subject. It was initially not a very exciting option for me!

At the end of the first year I realized that not only is water a truly fascinating subject but also that a water expert could make a far greater contribution to improve lifestyles and standards of living than a soil mechanic expert ever could dream. A few years later, I was totally convinced that this was the right decision for me. Life dealt me an ace, and I have never looked back!

More than two centuries ago, Samuel Taylor Coleridge wrote in his immortal poem, *The Rime of the Ancient Mariner*: "Water, water, everywhere, Nor any drop to drink." Coleridge's ancient mariner was stranded in the middle of an ocean on a motionless ship because there was no wind. The freshwater supply had run out. Thus, his statement was fully understandable. However, some 225 years after Coleridge wrote the poem, the situation in many parts of the world has become very similar to what was faced by the ancient mariner. The situation is now so grim that water from river and lakes and even underground water near the urban centres of the developing world cannot be drunk without significant treatment. According to the Third World Centre for Water Management, at least 3 billion people, and possibly as many as 3.6 billion people, still do not have access to clean drinking water. This is significantly higher than the entire population of the world when Coleridge wrote his remarkable poem.

Why has this happened in spite of the fact that scientific and technological developments have made tremendous progress over the past five decades, the world has been awash with money, the number of middle class households all over the world has increased to a level that is unprecedented in human history, and a true communication and information revolution has occurred all over the world? The answer, not surprisingly, is complex.

First, throughout history, water has been taken for granted. It has been used extensively and abused intensively without considering its future availability. One would be hard pressed to find a single country anywhere in the world where water has been managed efficiently and rationally for the past 30 years, let alone over a longer period. Not surprisingly, nearly all water sources in and around the urban centres of the developing world are under considerable stress, because of overuse as well as poor water quality management practices.

Second, sadly, throughout the world, one would be hard pressed to find a single country where political leaders have dealt with water issues seriously on a consistent basis over the past three to four decades. Leaders become interested in water only when there is a severe flood, a serious drought, or a calamitous natural hazard. Once the danger has passed, water no longer merits a place in their agendas. Yet, solutions to all water problems require long-term sustained attention: these cannot be resolved in three to four months, or even years.

Third, unlike other resources, water has a deep emotional linkage to human beings. It also has profound meaning and significance in all religions and cultures. It is the only natural resource people expect to be provided free or at highly subsidized prices. Water professionals claim that this is because human beings cannot survive without water. While this may be true, human beings also cannot survive and function without food, energy, and many other resources. Yet, no country provides food to everyone free or at very subsidized prices. Without energy, people will freeze to death in most temperate climates and mountainous areas. A city like Singapore cannot function without air conditioning which requires considerable energy. Yet, no one argues that energy or food should be provided free or with high subsidies.

The water mystique and emotionalism is evident too in the fact that no country wants to provide water to another country at any price, even when they may have water in excess of foreseeable needs. Take Canada. If any Canadian politician dares hint that there is excess water in the country and that this excess water could be exported to the United States at mutually agreed prices, that person would be committing political suicide! Countries will take other countries to WTO arbitration if they feel that their energy, agriculture, food, timber, or minerals cannot be freely exported. However, trade in water between countries, or even states within the same country (as in India and Pakistan), is unacceptable to the people and thus to politicians.

Fourth, water, in most countries of the world, is provided free. Agriculture, which accounts for nearly 65 percent of global water use, is provided free to all farmers everywhere in the world. Not surprisingly, farmers use much more water than they need, as a result of which in all countries where agriculture is an important activity, groundwater levels have been declining steadily as also river flows because of extensive water abstractions for irrigation. This situation can be noted in developed countries like the United States, France, Spain, and Australia as well as in most developing countries.

For domestic water use, prices are either free or subsidized in most places. Even in Singapore, where urban water management is one of the best in the world, the price of water has remained the same since 2000, while average household income has gone up by nearly 80 percent in the same period. Not surprisingly, an average Singaporean uses nearly 50 percent more water than a Hamburg resident, primarily because Hamburg has used water pricing very successfully as an instrument of water conservation and also has more innovative pricing policies. The absence of proper water pricing has been a major problem in water management all over the world.

Thus, the global water situation has been progressively worsened for the last several decades — not because there is not enough water in the world but rather because prevailing water management practices and processes have been consistently poor everywhere. Over the years they have improved only incrementally.

At present, not only are our management practices 30 to 40 years behind the times, but also many widely accepted facts and figures are significantly wrong and do not make much sense. When the accepted problem definitions are flawed, their solutions cannot be correct. In addition, the general public and policymakers do not appreciate the seriousness of the current and future water problems, especially when their magnitudes and extents have been consistently underestimated.

Take the oft-quoted 'fact' that the world has met its Millennium Development Goal (MDG) in water some three years before the target date. (The MDG stipulates that the number of people in the world who do not have access to safe water should be reduced by half between 1990 and 2015.) This achievement has been trumpeted by the United Nations as remarkable, especially when the majority of its targets in different areas are seldom met.

Let us consider the facts objectively and carefully. The United Nations Water Conference that was held in Mar del Plata, Argentina, in 1977, proposed that the decade of the 1980s should be considered as the International Water Supply and Sanitation Decade. By 1990, the target was that every person in the world should have water that is safe to drink. While this target proved to be over-ambitious like most other UN targets, the fact still remains that this decade was instrumental in providing clean water to millions of people all over the world who otherwise would not have had access to clean water.

However, the concept of "clean" or "safe" water was basically lost during the process. A cynic may claim that the process was deliberately fudged so that no matter what happens in reality, the target could be seen to be achieved. The two leading UN institutions, the WHO and UNICEF, came out with new terminology: the target was now referred to in terms of "improved" sources of water rather than "clean" or "safe". For all practical purposes, the WHO and UNICEF, who are responsible for monitoring progress in water supply and sanitation, allowed countries to define arbitrarily what constitutes "improved" sources of water. As a result, most developing countries decided to define "improved" as access to water, irrespective of its quality and quantity.

All UN institutions, the World Bank, and the regional development banks further obfuscated the problem by referring to "improved" sources of water at the beginning of their reports and then later consistently referring to "clean" or "safe" water. By using the terms "clean" or "safe" significantly more often than "improved" sources of water, international organizations have created an illusion that "only" 783 million people in the world "do not have access to clean water". For example, the UN trumpeted this "achievement" in its World Water Day message in 2013 and also in nearly all of its relevant publications.

The developing countries provided erroneous national data to the UN and the UN accepted these data without any qualms or questions and published such dubious information in their regular assessments because in the end both sides had an interest in claiming success. For example, *Progress in Drinking Water and Sanitation: 2013 Update* notes that Egypt had 100 percent piped water in all its urban premises in 2011. The figures for China were 95 percent, Mexico 94 percent, Congo 64 percent, and India 51 percent. An intelligent and perceptive tourist, who has spent even a week in any of these countries, would dispute these highly inflated, self-serving figures which are nowhere near the truth.

Let us consider South Asia as a whole, a region over 1.7 billion people. Neither the UN nor the countries of the region can showcase one reasonable-sized urban centre where the inhabitants dare drink directly from the taps. What is even worse is that in cities like Delhi or Dhaka, a decade ago people were using simple carbon filters to treat their water. In the intervening years, water pollution has become so severe that the citizens of these megacities are forced to use membranes before the water is safe to drink.

The world is subjected to similar misinformation in terms of sanitation targets. I was the principal advisor to the Secretary-General of the UN Water Conference and was one of the prime movers to have water supply and sanitation targets approved by this world body. When I proposed the targets for the Water Supply and Sanitation Decade (my suggestion was more modest), the idea was simple and unambiguous. Safe water was water which could be drunk without health concerns. Sanitation meant collecting wastewater from houses, treating it properly at a sewage treatment plant, and then discharging this treated wastewater safely to a water body without causing health hazards and environmental harms.

This simple definition was subsequently corrupted very significantly. Sanitation now means that households should have toilets and the wastewater needs to be taken out of the houses. What happens to the wastewater afterwards is not relevant! For instance, Delhi discharges nearly all its untreated wastewater into the Yamuna River and Mexico City exports its untreated wastewater to Mezquital Valley. Both megacities have been claiming for years that they have excellent sanitation!

Regrettably not only UN officials but also politicians all over the world are parroting grossly erroneous figures. Consequently, the consensus thinking at present is that the water supply and sanitation situation in the developing world is significantly better than it truly is on the ground. Even academics are not reading the fine print and are repeating erroneous facts. All these developments remind me of the infamous statement attributed to Joseph Goebbels: "If you tell a lie big enough and keep repeating it, people will eventually come to believe it." Sadly, the situation is somewhat similar in the water supply and sanitation areas.

The unfortunate fact is that given sustained political will, an informed public, and an alert media, there is absolutely no reason why any urban centre of more than 200,000 people cannot have a financially viable model to provide 24-hours of water that can be drunk straight from the tap. The domestic users of such a utility can pay for the water directly based on the exact amount of water they consume. Only the poor could receive a targeted subsidy to ensure that they have access to an adequate quantity and quality of water. By following this simple model, the city of Phnom Penh has already developed a world class water utility, many of whose performance indicators are better than those of London or Los Angeles. If a city like Phnom Penh, with all its current constraints and shortcomings, can achieve it, there is absolutely no reason why other Asian urban centres cannot duplicate this model with appropriate adaptations to account for local conditions.

As Marcel Proust said "The voyage of discovery is not in seeking in new landscapes but in having new eyes." In the area of water supply and wastewater disposal, the time has come — in fact I would argue long past — to look at these global problems with a new pair of eyes in order solve them. Recognizing the real dimensions of global water problems is my passion. Finding cost-effective, timely, and implementable solutions for them is my dream.

6 How Did I Get Here? Where am I Going? Thinking on a Bicycle

Joost BUURMAN

Like many Dutch I learned how to ride a bicycle shortly after I learned how to walk. My earliest memory of cycling is from primary school age. In the summer I rode to the edge of the village, right past the railway station, besides a long canal to meet my father on his way back from work. At the age of 12, I got my first roadbike, and my horizon expanded when I made long cycling trips through the landscape of Noord-Holland, a province of the Netherlands which lies largely below sea level. My favourite 37-kilometre trip ran 15 kilometres on top of a dike. On the right side was the wide, empty view of the IJsselmeer lake, and on the left side were green grasslands criss-crossed by straight canals. This was my natural habitat. I rode on dikes, passed canals, windmills, pumping stations and other water management infrastructure without giving it much thought. I just enjoyed the cycling to keep in shape and empty my mind.

I started studying economics at the height of a pig cycle, together with hundreds of first year students in the largest lecture theatres.[1] As I wanted to differentiate myself a bit from the finance and business economics crowd, I decided to study general economics in the second year, and by chance (filling up a two-hour gap in my lecture schedule) regional economics in the third year, ending up doing a fourth-year

---

1 The pig cycle describes cyclical fluctuations in supply. The classic reference is: M. Ezekiel, "The Cobweb Theorem," *The Quarterly Journal of Economics*, Vol. 52, No. 2 (Feb, 1938), 255–280.

specialisation in spatial economics and geographical information systems. I really enjoyed combining knowledge from two different disciplines, economics and geography, and realized that I am quite good at thinking in spatial terms. Besides finding my way back home without looking at a map on a cycling trip, I like to analyse problems with a spatial dimension.

With some more academic knowledge, I started to analyse the land use patterns I saw on my cycling trips. Especially in the western part of the Netherlands, the land use patterns are very strongly driven by water. In the early Middle Ages, the first settlements appeared on the highest grounds, which were old sandy creeks and levees built by men, resulting in long, stretched villages. Because the area flooded frequently, people joined forces and started building dikes. The fifteen-kilometre stretch of my favourite cycling trip is part of a circular dike of 126 kilometres completed in the year 1250 to protect 800 square kilometres of land. The idea of using windmills for water management surfaced in the 15th century, and in 1612 the first large lake, the Beemster, now a UNESCO heritage site, was reclaimed. Roads and canals follow a geometrical pattern in this area, which lies about four meters below sea level. Everything in the landscape is planned.

As I started travelling more, I encountered different types of landscapes. Vacation trips brought me to Belgium, France, Germany, Poland, England, and other European countries, and for an exchange programme I spent a semester at the university in Montpellier in the South of France, where I also brought my bicycle. Looking from train and plane windows and while doing my bicycle trips I observed land use patterns. In all places, you can see that historically access to water drove spatial planning. People founded villages and cities close to rivers or lakes that provided its inhabitants with freshwater. Water infrastructure, such as dams, canals and aqueducts, expanded the reach of settlements as civilisations developed. Still, access to water, or protection against too much water (floods) remained a key factor in explaining how land was used.

However, with advances in water engineering things have changed. Especially in the last century dams, pumping systems, desalination, and other engineering feats have allowed us to bring water to people, instead of locating people close to water. Think for instance of Las Vegas, a city that only could have grown so big due to the construction of the Hoover Dam; or cities in the Middle East that survive on desalinated water and deep groundwater. Engineering for too much water has also made large advances, with complex drainage systems and barrages for flood protection. It seems that this has disconnected people from water, and water seems no longer an important location criterion.

My first encounter with Asia was during a four-month internship with a project at the National Economic and Social Development Board in Bangkok at the end of my Master's studies. On the side-lines of a consulting project, I did a study of the relationship between development of roads and the location of industry. This study had nothing to do with water, but what I do remember are daily boat rides to the office over murky canals with a 'khlong taxi' and flooded areas near the Chao Praya river: in order to reach the jetty for the river taxi, you had to walk over makeshift boardwalks above ankle-deep water.

With my present-day knowledge, I have a much better understanding of the perilous situation that many low-lying cities are in. Massive groundwater extraction for drinking water and industrial use causes land to subside.[2] In addition, the natural sedimentation processes of floodplains that could offset some of the subsidence are no longer present in urbanized and developed areas. Asia has a large number of cities in this situation: Bangkok, Jakarta, Shanghai, and Ho Chi Minh City are just a few of the many. They are slowly sinking below sea level, a situation that a large part of the Netherlands is already in.[33]

Two years later an integrated coastal zone management project brought me again to Asia, this time Indonesia. With a team of researchers from various disciplines, such as marine biology, physical geography and political sciences, we studied the ecosystems in the Bay of Banten and the human pressures on these systems. This project made me realize the value of an interdisciplinary approach in studying policy-relevant problems. The small Bay of Banten was slated for industrialisation and port development. Only by working in a diverse team could we provide a

---

2　Besides groundwater extraction, there are other processes causing subsidence, such as natural consolidation of soils, though in many places groundwater extraction is the major cause of subsidence.

3　The Netherlands ended up for a large part below sea level due to consolidation of soils after building drainage systems, peat extraction, and reclamation of land below sea level, not so much due to groundwater extraction.

holistic understanding of the entire problem ranging from economic development to environmental protection.

In the mean time I had started a PhD on a project related to land use planning in the Netherlands. The study taught me many research skills, though the topic was more determined by the funding agency than by me. At some point, I was rather stuck with the study. On a grey, gloomy Sunday afternoon, I took my bicycle and cycled to the outskirts of Amsterdam, where the city meets the farmlands. The cycling trip cleared my mind, and I saw some ways to solve my PhD problems. From that point onwards, it was one more year of hard work and writing to complete the thesis.

My permanent relocation to Asia came when I decided to move to Vietnam after obtaining my PhD. My trips to Asia had made me realize that I preferred working in a less developed, more dynamic area than the Netherlands, where every square metre is planned and changes are marginal. In Vietnam, I worked on several projects related to river basins and flooding. Besides working on a large donor-funded integrated river basin management project for the Red River, I did a very interesting research project on the Mekong River.

The Mekong River has a very high biodiversity and still has a quite natural pattern of seasonal flooding of its floodplains, unlike many dammed rivers in the world. The high biodiversity, relatively natural state, and the fact that it crosses six fast developing countries, make it a rich study area. Economic development would require water infrastructure, for instance, building roads on levees to ensure access during the flood season and embankments around expanding cities to keep them dry. However, embankments can have irreversible impacts on the floodplains: some areas may no longer receive fertile sediments, and biodiversity may decline. In addition, large developments, such as hydropower dams, could have transboundary impacts. At first sight, these seem difficult trade-offs between economic development and environmental protection, though with creative thinking, economically and environmentally sustainable solutions can be found.

After four years in Vietnam, I moved to Singapore where I had the opportunity to join a collaborative project between the National University of Singapore and Deltares, a water research institute from the Netherlands. The focus of my work changed to urban water problems: in Singapore, there are no large river basins with complicated flood protection and water allocation problems. Although I worked more on research management than actual research, I learned a lot about urban water quality issues and the modelling of water quality and quantity. I also got involved in a land reclamation project, looking at economics and environmental impacts. As an added bonus, I could see one of my study areas develop on my weekend cycling trips: the Punggol-Serangoon Reservoir and Punggol Waterway. Working as a researcher on a project with the Institute of Water Policy made me again think about the relationship between people and water. Urbanites take it as given that water runs from their tap and their feet remain dry even during the heaviest downpours, without realizing the complex systems behind it and the trade-offs that need to be made. Even in modern cities, people depend on water supply and flood protection systems for their survival.

Recently, I had the opportunity again to cycle my favourite 37-kilometre trip near my parents' home. Cycling on top of the dike and overseeing the landscape, I thought about my research agenda at the Institute of Water Policy. It appeared to me that it is obvious to focus on flood and drought risk management. The pace of changes in the world is unprecedented, and many challenges have emerged in water management. In the past, it took many generations to build a solid dike to protect farmland, villages, and towns from flooding. In our times, flooding cannot be tolerated: it can be catastrophic for the large, fast-growing, and complex cities we now live in. At the same time, providing good quality water to all inhabitants of these cities is a great challenge. Add to that the dimensions of sustainable development and climate change and you have a large collection of research topics.

Water problems cannot be solved by a single discipline, but require collaboration between economists, sociologists, governance specialists, hydrologists, engineers, biologists, etc. Interdisciplinary research is traditionally difficult for highly focussed, specialized academics; and in general depth of knowledge scores better than breadth of knowledge in the academic world. Hence, from my perspective I can contribute to water management research by doing policy-relevant projects that foster collaborations between specialists and adding my perspective as an economist, with the aim of gathering and spreading knowledge to improve the large water projects carried out by governments, the World Bank, the ADB, and other organizations. The Institute of

Water Policy provides the perfect environment, with staff from different disciplines embedded in a university with hundreds of specialists in all kinds of fields. Exciting challenges lie ahead in studying embankments and flooding in India, comparing drought risk measures taken by cities around the world, determining the economic impacts of drought in Vietnam, helping governments with blue-green infrastructure development in cities, and many other related topics.

7 Is There a Macroeconomic Policy Regime in China?

CHEN Kang

Macroeconomic policies are arguably the most salient public policies, and they often exert a powerful influence on our daily lives. The exit from Quantitative Easing (QE) by the U.S. Federal Reserve and the introduction of a four trillion yuan stimulus package by the Chinese government, both of which have had a significant impact on the global economy in recent years, are just two such examples.

A macroeconomic policy regime is a systematic pattern of policy pursued by the authorities for macroeconomic management over the long run, reflecting the basic priorities (such as keeping inflation and unemployment low, maintaining exchange rate stability, or promoting economic growth) to which they are committed. It consists of foreign economic policy, monetary policy, fiscal policy, the financial system, and the institutional frameworks within which the economy operates.

It is not difficult to forget that China actually did not have a macroeconomic policy regime in 1978 when it started to embark on economic reform. As a centrally planned economy at the time, China did not have inflation because prices were fixed by the planners; there was no unemployment either because everybody was assigned a job; monetary policy was redundant in the mono-bank financial system; fiscal policy was subsumed under the planning mechanism, with firms, instead of paying taxes, surrendering all surpluses to the state; last but not least, China also sought to be self-sufficient during Mao's era, so the economy was closed to foreign trade and foreign investment, and there was no foreign economic policy to speak of.

All the above-mentioned conditions have changed as China is making the transition from plan to market. In less than four decades, the economy has been transformed beyond recognition. Millions have been lifted out of poverty, a moderately prosperous (or *xiaokang* in Chinese) economy has replaced one that was characterized by chronic shortages of consumer goods, and the Chinese people enjoy a level of economic freedom unprecedented in China's long history. However, inflation and unemployment, the two market miseries, have also returned and become the major concerns of China's policymakers.

How China conducts its macroeconomic policies to fight inflation and unemployment is not well understood. China's central bank frequently adjusts required reserve ratios of commercial banks or sells central bank papers in activities similar to open market operations conducted by the U.S. Federal Reserve, but it still controls interest rates, imposes credit ceilings, and issues administrative guidance. China's central government often adopts and implements anti-cyclical fiscal policies in typical Keynesian fashion, but it also requires local governments to fulfill annual growth targets in the same way as central planners dictated planning targets before the market reform. China has joined the WTO and become one of the most open economies in the world, and yet it still maintains capital control and has often been criticized for its heavy foreign exchange interventions.

Are there macroeconomic policy rules which have emerged from China's transition process? What are the basic priorities governing these rules? More fundamentally, is there a macroeconomic policy regime in China? How has it evolved, and how does it affect the behaviours of local governments and business firms? These are the research questions that greatly interest me.

It is obvious that the top priority of the Chinese government is to maintain high economic growth rates. The late Chinese leader Deng Xiaoping used to argue that "development is the only hard truth", because he believed that China's major problems, such as poverty, unemployment, and underemployment, could be resolved by economic development. Development was quantified into a number of key performance indicators (KPIs) for local government leaders, including growth rates of GDP, tax revenue collection, and foreign direct investment (FDI). Fulfilling the KPIs became one of the necessary conditions for the promotion prospects of local officials, who were incentivized thereby to do everything they could to meet growth targets, including engaging helpers outside the government.

While the proponents of the China Model like to portray the Chinese government as one that is capable of mobilizing huge amounts of fiscal resources to achieve almost any goal, my research points to two very different growth models at work in China (*China Models and Local Government Entrepreneurship 2013*). In the earlier years of the reform era, the role of the market was expanding, and local governments mainly played an enabling role in facilitating the growth of non-state sectors and following the demand-driven growth path to expand local tax bases under the revenue sharing system. It is only after 1998 that the current government-led investment-driven development model has gradually emerged, with local governments' focus being shifted towards rent seeking and monopolizing financial resources for their own investment projects.

It appears that all Chinese leaders are afraid of economic slowdowns — even if the slowdowns are for a short period of time. This was the main reason that forced the shift from China Model I to China Model II in the 1990s. When deflation in 1997–2002 threatened to destabilize the country, the technocrat leaders in Beijing, who were good at mobilizing government resources and never had a deep trust and understanding of market forces, quickly resorted to issuing administrative orders to local governments requiring them to guarantee at least 8 percent annual GDP growth within their region — or simply *baoba* in Chinese. *Baoba* ushered in the statist model of development in China characterized by "investment hunger".

Four underlying principles are implicit in *baoba*: (1) government at all levels, not market forces, should be responsible for economic growth; (2) resources, including fiscal and financial resources, should be reserved for governments to generate growth; (3) state-owned enterprises, which are closely linked with central and local governments, are important partners in *baoba* and should be given privileges or preferential treatment; and (4) local governments should guarantee economic growth even if economic, social, and environmental costs are high. Indeed, post-1998 China has followed these four principles closely in its economic expansion (*Rents and Rent Seeking in China 2014*). Currently, China's macroeconomic management is still preoccupied with the pro-growth priority, and the financial system is centred around this preoccupation and serving to mobilize resources, fiscal or extra-fiscal, for governments at various levels to produce GDP growth.

In another study (*How Are Exchange Rates Managed? 2012*), I looked at China's macroeconomic policy rules from a behavioural perspective. Central banks often intervene in the foreign exchange market to obtain desirable exchange rates, and how this is done has remained totally opaque. I think that central banks are likely to adopt a satisficing rather than optimizing strategy since they need to intervene frequently in a timely manner under conditions of incomplete information. I proposed a simple exchange rate management rule that spreads the volatilities originating from the anchor currencies among the exchange rates with the domestic currency. For example, I hypothesized that in managing foreign exchange rates the Chinese authorities are likely to adopt a heuristic that apportions the fluctuations of the Dollar-Euro rate between the RMB-Euro rate and the RMB-Dollar rate. By doing so, they have helped to soften the impact of exchange rate volatilities in key trading markets. My investigations show that the data is consistent with the proposed heuristics. Furthermore, when testing out this rule on nine additional currencies, I find the empirical evidence supports the proposed anchor-based policy rule as well.

In looking for monetary-policy rules, my initial studies concluded that China's money supply followed the Taylor rule fairly well up to 2008 and started to deviate from it after 2009. China's central bank, the People's Bank of China (PBOC), has also announced in recent years that they have decided to abandon Broad Money M2 as the monetary policy target and used instead the so-called "Total Social Financing" (TSF) which is considered to be a more representative measure. TSF, which is invented by PBOC, indicates the total funds the real economy obtains from the financial system over a certain period of time. My ongoing research is trying to understand how TSF and M2 affect each other in China's financial system and whether there are any policy rules emerging from the day-to-day policy practice.

This describes my main research activities in recent years. I am looking for the pieces of a puzzle before putting the puzzle together. The tricky thing is that the puzzle design keeps changing.

The Story of Missing Women

8

Yvonne J. CHEN

When I first started my research in applied microeconomics, many topics appeared inappropriate to me. I still remember the time I came across Emily Oster's article "Hepatitis B and the Case of Missing Women"[1]. I was furious about the fact that, as Professor Ha-Joon Chang once put it, economists are just trying to be everywhere! I even blogged about this and wrote, "To me this is a pure medical problem that can be, or ought to be, studied thoroughly in a controlled laboratory environment".

My research interest orients around observing and documenting human behaviour. In particular, I'm very curious about how individuals make decisions and how they interact with each other to reach a decision. The process of human decision-making is so complex that it involves researchers across a wide range of disciplines, neurologists, biologists, medical practitioners, and of course economists.

Oster's article makes me wonder what role economists play in science and in developing our understanding of the world around us. Economics is a study of markets and efficiency. Markets (and other related things) are tools used to allocate resources. Because there's resource scarcity, people start to think about efficiency and optimality. As a young researcher that has just started exploring the kaleidoscope of economic research, I think the primary and foremost important role for me is to document this resource allocation process.

1   Emily Oster ,"Hepatitis B and the Case of Missing Women", *Journal of Political Economy*, vol. 113(6), pp. 1163–1216, December 2005.

In order to fulfill this role, large amounts of data are needed. I've always considered data collection activities, especially longitudinal data sets, as an essential component of my responsibility as a researcher. The process of database building is usually long and tedious. However, the resources produced by this activity are fundamental to all kinds of economic research. I have been actively involved in many primary data collection projects, all of which took place in developing countries in Asia. I have participated in the large-scale China Household Finance Survey. The 2013 wave of the survey consists of 28,000 households and over 100,000 individuals. My co-author Namrata Chindarkar and I have designed and implemented a survey in rural Gujarat on women's employment and household relationships. We surveyed over 450 women and their husbands on all aspects of their family lives. We are also participated in an ongoing survey project in Kathmandu, in collaboration with the Institute of Water Policy (IWP) at our School, on water, time use, and health. The plan is to construct panel data by re-surveying the same 1,500 households after the completion of the Melamchi water project.

Now let me come back to the hepatitis B article. The question that kept puzzling me is what value an economist adds to this strand of research? An epidemiologist might tell you how many fetuses die from hepatitis B in a population. A biologist might tell you why the female fetus is more susceptible to hepatitis B. Biologists can explain the mechanisms, possibly at the cell level, through which the human immune system interacts with the virus. However, neither of them can tell nor predict the behavioural changes due to the correlation between hepatitis B and miscarriages. Simple evolutionary theories tell us that human beings alter their behaviours to adapt to environmental or social changes. For example, in some African tribes where there is a high death rate of boy infants due to a mysterious DNA trait, polygamy had become a dominating family structure in order to keep the population going. Similarly, in this case, as Oster pointed out, her primary interest was to study the compensating behaviours of families in the presence of the gender imbalance at birth due to hepatitis B. Do parents change their gender preference knowing that the virus reduces the probability of conceiving a girl? Do households nurture the girls better or worse knowing that hepatitis B and miscarriages are related? Such behavioural change and the reasons behind it are not the focus of standard epidemiological or biological studies. The channels and mechanisms underlying a human decision-making process can only be explored by close observation and careful documentation of changes in human behavioural patterns. From a policy perspective, it is critical for policymakers to build an expectation of behavioural responses when a policy is designed. We need to know how people would react to a policy before any recommendations can be made.

Amongst all the decision-making processes, I'm particularly interested in human capital related decisions, e.g. health and education. Human capital is illiquid and non-transferrable, which distinguishes it from other types of assets or capital. The investment and return cycle is usually very long and subject to liquidity constraints, especially in developing countries. In many cases, health and education investments for young children are made by their parents. The analysis of these problems therefore requires a basic assumption about not only individual preferences and utility functions but also dynastic models and intergeneration transfer patterns. And many of these decision-making processes are subject to local social norms and culture, which are difficult to define and quantify.

The complications in human capital ignite my interest in this topic. In a study that I did on China, my co-authors and I explored the relationship between the Confucians social norm of supporting old age parents and human capital investment as well as patterns of intergenerational transfers. We found that parents in regions with a higher presence of the Confucianism social norm invest more in children's education and save less. Meanwhile, these parents also receive more support from their adult children when they retire. These findings indicate that human capital investments in children present some features of a commercial loan, which refutes the prevailing hypothesis that parents are completely altruistic when it comes to child bearing.[2]

Compared to individual or household decision-making, decision-making as a group is even more difficult to characterize. How do individuals interact with each other till a consensus is reached? To answer this question, again, a large amount of data is needed. Usually a census of the interested population is required. Namrata

---

2   Yvonne J. Chen, Zhiwu Chen and Shijun He,"Confucianism, Social Norms and Saving Rates in China", Working Paper, 2014.

Chindarkar and I are starting a new project on social network and women's empowerment in rural areas. We hope to open up the black box of a household's bargaining process by studying the patterns of information dissemination in villages.

The missing women story ends with a twist. Oster's paper stirred up a huge debate in the literature due to controversies over the data. She herself wrote a follow-up article acknowledging that there was an error in the original analysis.[3] Although this is not the Hollywood happy ending that we all expect, her paper certainly added to my understanding of economic research as a profession.

I'd like to end this essay with my favourite quote from Bertrand Russell, which has guided my odyssey in research so far, "When you are studying any matter, or considering any philosophy, ask yourself *only* what are the facts and what is the truth that the facts bear out. Never let yourself be diverted either by what you wish to believe, or by what you think would have beneficent social effects if it were believed. But look only, and solely, at what are the *facts*."[4]

---

3 Emily Oster (with Gang Chen et al, "Hepatitis B Does Not Explain Male-Biased Sex Ratios in China", *Economics Letters*, 107(2): p. 142–144, May 2010.

4 "Love Is Wise, Hatred Is Foolish: Bertrand Russell on Rationality and Tolerance", BBC Interviews, 1959.

9 Why Public Policy Needs to Take a Broader View on Well-Being

Namrata CHINDARKAR

How should poverty be conceptualized? Why is it important to expand women's labour market opportunities? How does investment in water infrastructure affect households and individuals? Thinking as a traditional economist, one would respond that poverty and inequality are essentially about income or monetary deprivation; expanding women's labour market opportunities can enable them to increase their own as well as their household's consumption; and investments in water infrastructure can significantly increase household productivity. While these responses are accurate from the perspective of standard microeconomic theory and most policy-makers would aim to achieve precisely these objectives, I argue that a broader view of well-being is necessary to make more informed policy decisions.

Conventional economic theory relies on the decision utility as being the primary determinant of well-being. It argues that 'rational' human beings aim to maximize utility by making preferences and choices subject to a given budget constraint. The emphasis is on revealed preferences which can be objectively observed and measured. These choice decisions determine individual well-being. Recently however, 'experienced utility' has been brought into the discussion (Kahneman et al., 1997). Following Clark et al. (2008), I represent this expanded notion of utility using a simple utility function,

$$U = U(u_1(Y)), u_2(T - L), u_3(P))$$

In the above equation U is the combined utility, which is made up of three sub-utility functions. $u_1(Y)$ is the utility derived from income or consumption[1]; $u_2(T-L)$ is the utility gained from leisure; and $u_3(P)$ is the experienced utility typically captured using subjective or psychological measures. Together, these form the sources of individual well-being.

A cynical policymaker might ask, "I am only concerned with my people maximizing $u_1(Y)$. Why are $u_2(T-L)$ and $u_3(P)$ of policy concern?" This is a valid question, and I will attempt to convince this cynical policymaker using emerging theory and evidence and my own research work in three development policy areas — (i) poverty, (ii) gender and employment, and (iii) improved access to water. Following the expanded notion of utility, my research takes a two-pronged approach on well-being. In addition to examining the monetary aspects such as income and consumption, I delve into the non-monetary aspects such as time-use, life satisfaction, and health.

Looking first at the issue of poverty and inequality, conventional wisdom on this topic has been that it is only income driven. However, recent research provides evidence that poverty has negative psychological consequences and impedes the cognitive ability of the poor thus leading them to make irrational decisions which in turn perpetuate poverty (Mani et al., 2013, Haushofer and Fehr, 2014). This new evidence raises at least two crucial questions for policymakers — (i) should poverty alleviation policies be aimed at reducing the negative psychological consequences of poverty and (ii) how can the poor be assisted in making rational economic decisions?

In my research, I have attempted to address the first question by examining the psychological effects of different poverty alleviation programmes, specifically, livelihood protecting programmes such as in-kind transfers and livelihood promoting programmes such as microfinance. I find that poverty alleviation programmes such as microfinance, which focus on self-reliance, have positive psychological effects on the beneficiaries. On the other hand, in-kind transfer programmes result in negative psychological effects, which I argue is plausibly owing to "welfare stigma". Such research is likely to provide crucial insights to policymakers to choose poverty

---

1   In a model without savings, income and consumption would be equal.

alleviation policies that can both increase income and reduce the negative psychological effects, which might perpetuate poverty.

Next, let's consider utility gains from providing access to skilled labour opportunities to women, especially those from low-income households and possessing low human capital. A policy problem in India is that of dismally low female labour force participation. It has been argued that this is not only because of social constraints but also because of lack of skills development and limited opportunities outside of the agricultural sector. Exploiting a natural experiment from a unique training and alternative employment programme for low-income and low-human capital women in Gujarat, I examine the effect of this programme on women's intra-household bargaining ability.[2] Intra-household bargaining is operationalized in terms of increased personal consumption, control over consumption decisions, and experienced utility outcomes such as life satisfaction and aspirations. Interestingly, I find that the programme leads to an increase in women's expenditure on jewelry, control over household spending, and overall life satisfaction. This is significant from a policy perspective as the experienced utility gained from skilled employment plays an equally significant role in keeping women in the labour force and encouraging others to participate.

And finally, let's examine the effect of improved access to water on households and individuals.[3] In developing countries such as India and Nepal access to sufficient and good quality water remains an unresolved issue. Preliminary research in Gujarat and the Kathmandu Valley suggests that this affects economic activities as well as imposes a huge cost on the time-use and experienced utility of women and children, who are often responsible for collecting for the household. Focus group discussions with households in the Kathmandu Valley revealed that owing to the unreliable water supply, time is shifted away from economically productive activities and leisure (such as spending time with family and pursuing personal interests) towards water collection. The daily struggle to meet the household's water requirements also results in stress and conflict within and between households. Further, insufficient and poor quality water has a severe negative effect on health outcomes,

---

2   Joint research with Dr. Yvonne J. Chen, Assistant Professor, Lee Kuan Yew School of Public Policy.
3   Joint research with the Institute of Water Policy, Lee Kuan Yew School of Public Policy.

which decreases productivity and shifts income away from other productive uses. Therefore, the negative effects on leisure and experienced utility are just as significant as the effect on economic production as they directly affect quality of life, which is clearly a public policy objective.

In summary, I would tell the cynical policymaker that maximizing $u_2(T-L)$ and $u_3(P)$ does not substitute $u_1(Y)$ as the primary policy objective. Rather, policymakers can gain valuable complementary insights into the effects of public policy on households and individuals by examining a broader set of sub-utility functions. This framework can be extended to understand a range of policy issues such as the effect of household financial planning, social safety nets, tax reforms, and unemployment benefits.

To conclude, I would like to quote from one of my all-time favourite readings, *The Hitchhiker's Guide to the Galaxy*. "What is the answer to the ultimate question of life, the universe, everything?" asked the hyper-intelligent, pan-dimensional beings. Readers continue to grapple with this question and have responded with ideas ranging from mathematical algorithms to philosophical discussions on existentialism. However, in my opinion, the most relevant answer is 'well-being'. It is indeed true that the central purpose of human life and existence is to seek well-being whether through a well-paying and gratifying job, increased consumption, setting up a comfortable home, or spending time with and having aspirations for the family. All of these are directly influenced by public policy, and therefore there is a need for policymakers and policy researchers to embrace a broader conception of well-being.

References

Clark, A., Frijters, P., and Shields, M. (2008). "Relative Income, Happiness, and Utility: An Explanation for the Easterlin Paradox and Other Puzzles." *Journal of Economic Literature*, 46(1), 95–144.

Haushofer, J. and Fehr, E. (2014). "On the Psychology of Poverty." *Science*, 344(6186), 862–867.

Kahneman, D., Wakker, P., and Sarin, R. (1997). "Back to Bentham? Explorations of Experienced Utility." *Quarterly Journal of Economics*, 112, 375–405.

Mani, A., Mullainathan, S., Shafir, E., and Zhao, J. (2013). "Poverty Impedes Cognitive Function." *Science*, 341(6149), 976–980.

10 From Slobodan Milosevic to Doraemon

HENG Yee Kuang

Over dinner one night at a *chanko nabe* restaurant in central Tokyo (where sumo wrestlers traditionally go to bulk up their bodies), a journalist with Japan's Kyodo News Agency once asked me how it was that I ended up doing research on both 'hard' and 'soft' power topics. Both my journalist friend and I did not succeed in significantly bulking up our bodies that night, but my answer in retrospect was a curious mix of images representing both extremes of perceived brutality and saccharin sweetness in international politics: former Yugoslav President Slobodan Milosevic and iconic Japanese cartoon character, *Doraemon.* Let me explain.

As an undergraduate student living in London, I experienced for the first time how elections can trigger sweeping changes in the political mood of a major Western country like the United Kingdom. As he swept into Downing Street surrounded by Union Jack-waving well-wishers in May 1997, a time of high optimism, the newly elected British Prime Minister Tony Blair stated: "Mine is the first generation able to contemplate the possibility that we may live our entire lives without going to war or sending our children to war." Yet, as a student of International Relations, I wondered even then if exuberance had gotten to the head of the otherwise reasoned Blair.

Fast forward to May 1999: sitting in my tiny room in my university hall of residence, I recall vividly straining my eyes to watch a tiny portable TV set carrying 'live' images of British warplanes taking off to strike targets in Kosovo as NATO attempted to reverse the ethnic cleansing allegedly orchestrated by Milosevic. This was the summer exam season at the London School of Economics, and while studying for my 'Ethics of War' module, I found myself more drawn to the TV set than my tomes of books about the philosophers of war. Kosovo was a rather curious little sort of 'war' where the Western allies in NATO had gone to extraordinary lengths to ensure the safety of their deployed military personnel fighting in a corner of Europe which was not even part of NATO. As the campaign wore on with little visible success, military intervention was justified to a sceptical public as a 'new' type of humanitarian intervention.

The lecture hall of another of my modules, 'Strategic Aspects of International Relations', was crammed full to the brim, and students were even happy to sit on the floor. I was surprised to learn that most in the audience were in fact not formally enrolled in the module itself. As I attempted to apply what I had learnt in my ethics classes such as the doctrine of 'double-effect' to real-world events in Kosovo, I gradually realized that war and conflict retained a fascination in the human psyche even in liberal, post-modern Europe. Yet, war was no longer what Britain had become accustomed to, despite its unfortunately long experience of it. Mass celebrations of heroism, sacrifice and glory were replaced by media criticism of Blair and the mission; the quintessentially British notion of a 'wobble' in public opinion; and for me above all, an overriding obsession with minimizing and reducing all sorts of risks: of the conflict spreading; to the loss of allied pilots; to the unfortunately termed collateral damage of civilian casualties.

Thankfully, my many hours glued to watching grainy green and white images of bombs hitting their targets did not inflict long-term damage to my prospects, and I managed to earn a British Government Overseas Research Scholarship to conduct doctoral studies on the role of risk in the transformation of war. Events after Kosovo, notably the 9/11 attacks in New York and the resulting US war on terror and invasion of Iraq, not only crystallized for me the centrality of managing risk in emerging Western strategic thought. The post-9/11 period introduced the world to concepts such as 'unknown unknowns' uttered by US Defence Secretary Donald Rumsfeld in his attempt to explain the US rationale for invading Iraq. When the UK Plain English

Campaign presented Rumsfeld with the 'Foot in the Mouth Award 2003' for the most 'baffling comment made by a public figure', this was seen as a form of ridicule.

In our PhD student research rooms overlooking the Strand, I still distinctly remember the noise as the largest anti-war protests in British history took to the streets. However, for students of risk like me, Rumsfeld made perfect sense in his strategic logic, for he had touched on one of the classic policy dilemmas of risk: how to decide in the face of uncertain knowledge when the stakes could be enormously high? Looking back on Tony Blair's initial optimism about his generation's lack of experience of war, it seems ironic now that he in fact became known as the British Prime Minister who had taken the country to war most frequently during his tenure, often based on what I would term the logic of risk management.

Undertaking research on the intersections between risk studies and International Relations, I have since completed my PhD dissertation on risk; published two books on the role of risk in strategy and international security; and several peer-reviewed journal articles on the topic. I have also been an invited guest speaker on these topics at military staff colleges and defence academies from Denmark and Finland to Japan and Singapore.

My first academic position after completing my PhD was to prove another unexpected watershed in my research trajectory. As a newly appointed lecturer at Ireland's oldest and most prestigious university, Trinity College Dublin, I was asked to host a lecture and visit to the campus by Japan's Ambassador to Ireland, who had a laudable proactive policy of trying to engage as much as possible with academic institutions. H.E. Hayashi Keiichi, one of Japan's most accomplished diplomats, would go on to serve as Deputy Vice Minister and Assistant Chief Cabinet Secretary, and then Ambassador to the United Kingdom. Through the course of H.E Hayashi's visit and lecture, my interest in Japanese foreign policy was sparked, particularly how a country widely perceived to be in relative decline would attempt to marshal its resources in the face of a rising neighbour like China.

Serving on the Royal Irish Academy's National Committee for the Study of International Affairs, I was then asked to pen an article on Japan's power capabilities vis-a-vis China's. Around this time, it was reported that Japan's *Gaimusho* (Ministry of Foreign Affairs) had plans to launch its first-ever *anime* ambassador to boost

Japan's global profile, the lovable robotic cartoon cat character *Doraemon,* who can travel through time and loves Japanese Dorayaki beanpaste pancakes. Rather incredulous and curious as to why otherwise dour bureaucrats at MOFA had now turned to harnessing this cartoon character of whom I had fond memories during my childhood, this was when I began studying 'soft' power in Japan's foreign policies: my entry point to more Asian-focused research when I moved to assume a new tenured position at the 600 year-old University of St Andrews in Scotland, the fabled home of golf and alma mater of the Duke and Duchess of Cambridge, Prince William and Catherine Middleton.

I received grants to conduct research on soft power and, with H.E Hayashi's encouragement and assistance, was able to gain access to interview Gaimusho officials in charge of public diplomacy and soft power. Japan's soft power resources are varied, and studying each of these dimensions from its environmental policies to cultural appeal and peacekeeping missions has proven productive. I have published a co-edited book, book chapters, and several peer-reviewed journal articles on this topic. Perhaps most satisfying of all in terms of peer recognition, I have also been invited to speak at the University of Tokyo and other institutions in Japan such as the National Institute of Defence Studies.

The latest stage of my research development coincided with my relocation to NUS for mostly family-related reasons, but research has also proven to be exciting. Based in a dynamic global city like Singapore where policymakers constantly warned of the country's vulnerability to security challenges such as SARS and cyber-attacks, I wondered how my research agenda on risk and globalization could fit into this new setting. Supported by a generous and conducive research environment, I launched a project to examine the linkages between hyper-connected global cities and their exposure to rapidly spreading global risks. Singapore, and NUS in particular, is an ideal setting to study interconnectivity and the downsides of globalization. As NUS is a partner of the World Economic Forum's Global Risks Report, I was asked to participate in the development of risk cases for the 2013 report.

This experience further convinced me that interconnectivity and global shocks will define the world of the future, especially for tiny, highly-connected global cities like Singapore. Based on my research findings, I have since published a peer-reviewed article and revised another on Singapore's experience of global risks as a global city and am finishing off what would be my fourth book, to be published in 2015.

Working in a public policy school also means engaging with colleagues from other disciplines. Singapore again provides a useful impetus for research, particularly on urbanization and globalization. Speaking with younger colleagues about their research agendas has been particularly eye-opening, exposing me to ideas and theories I had not learnt of but that could prove useful to our research. As a result, I have been involved in inter-disciplinary collaborative projects with colleagues working together on Asia's global cities, bringing together insights and theories from Public Administration, Urban Studies, and International Relations.

Over the years, my research has expanded both geographically (from an Anglo-American focus to an Asia-Pacific outlook on Japan and Singapore) and thematically (from risk in strategic studies to the study of soft power in Asia). This has been driven both by events and personalities as well as my own personal curiosity in an increasingly complex world. In years to come, as renewed interest in Japan's global security profile grows under Abenomics, I believe that various dimensions of soft power can help to explain how Japan seeks to engage the world and how the world perceives Japan. Normative power is one future avenue I am exploring, in conjunction with colleagues based in Australia. I also hope to merge my two pre-existing research trends, particularly through what I call the 'Asianisation' of risk studies which has so far largely been dominated by European scholars and European policy concerns.

However, recently I have been invited to participate in a new research initiative on risk based at the University of Tokyo, and I look forward to launching projects, particularly comparative analyses of risk: how it is conceptualized; how it manifests in policy-making; and how risk management is implemented in both Singapore and Japan. This does not mean turning my back on risk in the British and American context. To the contrary, I continue to have deep links and interests on how risk is being institutionalized in the UK, especially through the National Risk Registers and the National Security Strategy. Studying these developments in the UK also allows scholars working in Asia to have a better understanding of how these might in turn apply to their own needs, whether in Japan or Singapore.

11 The Poetry of Politics: What I Research and Why

Selina HO

Where the mind is without fear and the head is held high;
Where knowledge is free;
Where the world has not been broken up into fragments
By narrow domestic walls; Where words come out from the depth of truth;
Where tireless striving stretches its arms towards perfection;
Where the clear stream of reason has not lost its way
Into the dreary desert sand of dead habit;
Where the mind is led forward by thee
Into ever-widening thought and action
Into that heaven of freedom, my Father, let my country awake.

Where the Mind Is Without Fear, Rabindranath Tagore, written in 1910 and
translated into English in 1912

Rabindranath Tagore's famous poem is not just a rallying call for his country, but also touches on the themes of universalism, freedom of knowledge, freedom from fear, the primacy of reason and truth, and the centrality of action. These are the values that inspire me to conduct research in the field of politics and international relations, as I seek to understand the world we live in, with its complex web of inter-state and intra-state relations.

In particular, a fascination with Chinese history since an early age has led to an abiding interest in contemporary issues related to China. I also became interested in developing an in-depth understanding of the linkage between resource issues and security issues, as a result of the new sets of security concerns that have arisen because of resource competition around the world. As a former public servant, I fully appreciate the real-world implications of these issues. At the same time, my transition to academia is prompted by an interest in theory development and an admiration for academic rigour.

As a graduate student in the Johns Hopkins University School of Advanced International Studies (SAIS), I developed an interest in the study of the developmental state and bureaucratic politics. My doctoral dissertation is broadly based on the question of whether China is a classic East Asian developmental state like South Korea, Japan, and Taiwan. My answer is that while China in many respects resembles a developmental state, it is nevertheless different from South Korea, Japan, and Taiwan; China lacks a clear state-directed industrial policy and strong old boys' network, both of which are critical to the success of the other East Asian countries in the 1980s. China is also larger than the other East Asian countries, and as a result, the interactions between China's central government and local governments have a more profound impact on governance. It is therefore more meaningful in China's case, to speak of local developmental models, as different localities have adopted different models of growth.

My dissertation examines how the developmental models of three cities — Beijing, Shanghai, and Shenzhen — impact the structure and performance of their municipal water sectors. It explains why despite having an urban water management framework that has been upheld as a nation-wide model, Shenzhen is the least efficient (in relative terms) of the three cities in terms of water service provision; it has the highest per capita daily tap water consumption for residential use and the highest proportion of water loss among the three cities.

I am currently revising my dissertation to produce a book manuscript that compares public goods provision in China and India, focusing specifically on the municipal water sectors in both countries. Studies have shown that the level of public goods provision is higher in democratic systems than authoritarian forms of government. This is because democracies produce policies that result from political processes which aggregate citizen preferences whereas authoritarian governments need only cater to the small group in power.

Public goods provision in China and India, however, appears to buck against conventional wisdom; whether in terms of access to education, healthcare, electricity, public transportation, and clean water, China does consistently better than India. Using empirical evidence from the Chinese and Indian municipal water sectors, my book manuscript explains why authoritarian China performs better than democratic India in providing public goods. Do types of political regimes affect government performance in public goods provision? What is unique to China and India that explain their performance outcomes in providing water to urban residents? My study shows that administrative structures, political cultures, fears of social instability, quality of leadership, quality of local governments, rule of law and accountability, and rural-urban migration policies are perhaps more important than types of political systems in determining how well governments provide public services.

Apart from this project, I am also working on a second research project on how resource competition shapes relations between rising powers and between rising powers and established powers. Empirical observations of the behaviour of rising powers in resource competition will not only facilitate theory development on rising powers in international relations but are also of high practical value in helping the international community develop policies that will encourage rising powers to abide by international norms.

In the first phase of this project, I have written an article on "River Politics: China's Policies in the Mekong and the Brahmaputra in Comparative Perspective," in the *Journal of Contemporary China* (online version in July 2013 and print version in January 2014). It asks the question why China is relatively more cooperative in the Mekong than in the Brahmaputra. It discusses the role of domestic actors as well as the geopolitics of the Southeast and South Asian regions in shaping Chinese behaviour. Power asymmetries and historical relations between China and the other riparian states are two key factors explaining the different levels of Chinese cooperation. My article also examines the political and security implications of Chinese behaviour in managing its international rivers, which are invaluable sources of hydropower, in its relations with India and Indochina. In addition, I have recently written a book chapter on China's transboundary policies towards India (forthcoming), which examines the prospects for cooperation between China and India on the Brahmaputra River. In line with the broader themes of China-India relations, I have also written a book chapter on China's shifting perceptions of India (forthcoming).

In the second phase of my second research project, I have completed an article related to resource competition among rising powers, entitled "China's and India's Investments in Africa: Complementarity, Competition, and Collaboration?" This article examines whether China and India's economic activities in Africa are necessarily zero-sum or whether there are signs that the two rising powers have adopted strategies that complement each other. I rely on sets of data from the UNCTAD, Heritage Foundation, and the Statistical Bulletins of China's Overseas Foreign Direct Investment (published by the Chinese Ministry of Commerce) for my analysis. My study shows that it is inaccurate to portray Chinese and Indian interactions in Africa as either competing or cooperative. Instead, they are simultaneously competing and collaborating with each other. In the process, they are also learning from each other's business practices in Africa. This article has been submitted to a peer-reviewed journal.

In order to holistically understand how resource competition affects the behaviour of rising powers, it is imperative to examine how resource competition affects regional stability. As a pilot to this long-term project, I have recently proposed an international conference on water politics and regional stability that examines how competition for water around the world affects relations among riparian states. At the minimum, water diversions and dam construction have the effect of generating tensions between upstream and downstream riparians. In the worst-case scenario, cutting off a country's water supply is a *casus belli*. Papers presented at this conference will be compiled into an edited volume for publication. The longer-term goal is to institutionalize an annual conference that examines the impact of resource and environmental issues on regional stability.

My ruminations on the final phases of my second research project on rising powers and resource competition have yet to take concrete shape. Broadly speaking, I intend to compare the historical cases of Japan and Germany with the contemporary cases of China and India. Some questions I would like to ask include: in what ways are China and India similar to Japan and Germany, and in what ways are they different? As the resource competition among China, India, the United States, and Japan has tremendous implications for regional and global security, as well as environmental sustainability, how do China and India interact with the established powers in their quest for resources? Are there parallels with pre-World War Two Japan and Germany? How do China's and India's resource-seeking behaviour impact the international system today?

12 Tracing How Governments Think

Michael HOWLETT

Many observers of policy-making processes tend to be quite cynical about how governments operate. Not in terms of whether or not a government can do good in society — which most firmly believe to be possible — but in terms of its ability to think 'rationally': that is, to articulate clear goals and find and implement the means to achieve them in an efficient and effective way. This is a view which is not restricted to the sometimes poorly-informed general public. Political scientists and economists, for example, having studied in detail how bureaucracies and legislatures operate in practice, are often very skeptical of the idea that a large complex organization such as a government can "think" in the same way as can a person — who often has more or less only one interest to serve and only one mind to convince as to the best course of action to follow in achieving a goal. Instead, they find governments to be composed of many interests and factions and their actions surrounded by very high degrees of uncertainty and ambiguity: that is, uncertainty of goals and ambiguity in how to achieve them. In such circumstances, governments have been likened to 'black boxes', or more prosaically, "sausage factories", in which somewhat mysterious processes unfold — from bargaining to log-rolling and compromise — which lead to the production of actions (policies) that do not necessarily contain any coherence or consistency or logic of purpose in the way individuals or smaller organizations might articulate and achieve them.

This view is very problematic for the policy sciences which, since the earliest work of Harold Lasswell in the 1940s and 1950s, have been based on the idea that knowledge can be mobilized by governments to better achieve their aims and ambitions, implying a more instrumental or 'rational' process of policy formulation and decision-making than is often observed. In some cases, this has led policy scientists, and others, to despair of governments ever achieving any kind of optimality in their policy efforts and to urge strategies of decision involving only minimal changes from the status quo which, they argue, are less likely to do harm than more active alternatives which ignore the inability of governments to think in a rational way.

But this conservatism is not equitable in the sense that it leaves many large problems from climate change to poverty reduction and sustainable development, and those affected by them, without recourse to the use of the state and state resources to tackle these issues. And, as critics of such incremental strategies have pointed out, while evidence of incompetence and irrationality abounds in government behaviour, there is also ample evidence of governments, despite their complexity, being able to conduct themselves instrumentally: designing and adopting appropriate mixes of tools to address major problems such as space exploration, wars, public health and disease control, and the development and operation of transportation and utilities infrastructure, to name only a few.

The latter point is especially significant because it suggests the problem of irrationality is not inherent to government, per se, but rather that certain conditions and activities within the 'black box' of policy formulation sometimes operate to allow more instrumental rationality to permeate policy-making. And one of the major challenges and research agendas in the policy sciences is to try to better understand the formulation and decision-making processes in general, and more specifically with respect to policy success and failure, in order to promote improved or enhanced policy outcomes.

This is a research agenda which has concerned both academics and practitioners in recent years in the study of what some have termed 'policy work' and 'policy advice', such as those involved in the 'evidence-based policy movement' in sectors like health and education who are dedicated to understanding and improving policy-making processes and ensuring that the results of the latest clinical trials and investigations inform policy-making practice. But it is not restricted to this group or only to these one or two large sectors.

I have been very fortunate over the past two years in my capacity as Yong Pung How Chair Professor to have been able to work on a continuing basis with LKY School colleagues in pursuing several research projects related to this ongoing agenda. These efforts have centred on research into several topics that have concerned us over the past decade but whose time for study always seemed to be overtaken by shorter-term priorities and needs. They have included looking into topics such as "Policy Design", "Good Governance", "Policy Failures", "Policy Capacity", and "Dealing with Ambiguity and Uncertainty" which we have thought about, questioned and, thanks to the excellent research environment of the School, have attracted the best minds internationally to discuss and investigate.

Thanks to the research programmes available at the School, over the past two years my LKY School colleagues and I have been able to mount international work-shops on the first four topics in Singapore and China and are currently planning a fifth workshop to deal with the last topic. The workshops have brought together leading authors from around the world and Asia and have resulted in a series of dynamic discussions which have advanced thinking on the subject of 'how governments think'. They have helped to clarify the processes and activities involved in policy design, assessed the nature of different modes of governance and what constitutes good governance in each, and have clarified the programme, political, and process issues which are involved in determining policy success and failure. They have also clarified the many competences and capabilities which governments need to operate at a high level and how those capabilities and competences have shifted over time.

The result has been a series of high-quality publications including edited vol-umes from leading academic presses and special issues in highly-ranked journals including *Policy Sciences*, *Journal of Comparative Policy Analysis*, *Public Policy and Administration*, *Policy & Politics and Policy & Society* which will be appearing throughout 2014–2016 and which promise to spark and inform the debate on these issues within academe as well as affect policy practices in the field.

LKY School colleagues are now pursuing further research into each of these topics. I have been focusing most of my efforts on better defining and understanding 'policy design' as a specific form of policy formulation. This is a long-term project which has involved co-authors and collaborators in Hong Kong (HKU), Canada (JSGSPP), New York (NYU), Paris (Science Po), Berlin, the UK, and elsewhere with whom I have been collaborating on a series of projects and publications re-examining the existing academic literature on policy design from the 1970s, 1980s, and 1990s, updating it to take into account recent developments in policy theory and practice. These have included projects and publications examining insights gained from behavioural economics ("nudging"), distinguishing design from 'non-design' in policy formulation, examining how best to design complex portfolios of tools to deal with problems ("policy mixes") as well as dealing with concerns about temporality and its impact on design spaces (affecting policy change through processes such as "layering" or "drift"). The work involves PhD and post-doctoral students and fellows at NUS and in Canada and is continuing with new projects underway. Amongst the new projects is the study of activities undertaken by key actors in policy advisory systems who advocate particular solutions regardless of the problem to be addressed ("instrument constituencies"). Another examines how policymakers design policies with the adaptability and resilience needed to deal with long-term and multi-faceted issues, such as climate change.

Policy design work is interesting not only academically but also for practitioners who must face the challenge of designing and adapting policy tools and instruments to meet new and existing problems on a day-to-day basis. One of the initiatives which we have undertaken at the LKY School to help with this aspect of policy work has been to create a "Policy Design Lab": an on-line source of information and news for practitioners about developments in governments and academe dealing with these subjects. The Design Lab (http://policy-design.org) has partnered with other NUS bodies such as the Institute for Water Policy (IWP) and the LKY School on research projects and conferences to help think about policy tools and design issues in areas such as water policy and social policy and will continue to do so in the coming years.

Taken together these projects have helped create and solidify the community of university, government, and civil society-based analysts in Asia and globally who are concerned with improving policy designs and outcomes. While much more work remains to be done, it has been a very good start, and I am looking forward to continuing these efforts over the next several years.

13 The Challenge for Labour Market Policy Research

HUI Weng Tat

The success of Singapore as an economic miracle has been attributed to its sound and pragmatic policies and the existence of a disciplined, industrious, and trained quality workforce.

I am a beneficiary and by-product of this early emphasis on the development of quality human capital. I experienced first-hand, as one of the pioneer batch of students, the introduction of technical education in the mainstream secondary school curriculum and the focus on engineering subjects in pre-university classes. These were part of the strategic human development policies to attract and complement the inflow of multinational investments in industry which helped spur Singapore's rapid economic growth. The award of a Colombo Plan undergraduate scholarship from Australia enabled me to make my first overseas trip which ultimately led to a career in academia.

Having been born and raised in an environment that placed great emphasis on labour as a highly-treasured resource for the nation, it was not surprising that I was drawn to the fascinating subject of labour economics and studying the factors that would contribute to labour's effective deployment and efficient utilization. My early years in research were focussed on mastering the technical aspects of economic optimization and modelling techniques. I was fortunate to gain access to the first wave of an Australian panel data set, which introduced me to panel data econometrics used in the modelling and analysis of labour market transitions of labour force participants. This was the focus of my PhD thesis.

My academic life began when I was granted permission to serve out the remaining period of my undergraduate scholarship bond (1986–1991) at the National University of Singapore. Being situated in Singapore however also meant that it was no longer possible, given the state of technology at the time, to continue to do research with panel or local micro-level data sets. To this day, such data are still not made available to independent researchers outside government service. The dearth of rich micro-data sets led to a reluctant shift in research to the analysis of the labour market using aggregated macro-data and into the wider world of labour market policies and issues. It also led to a subsequent move from teaching in a mainstream economics department to becoming part of the engaging multidisciplinary environment at the Lee Kuan Yew School of Public Policy.

My early research was centred primarily on the role of foreign labour and its contribution to and impact on the Singapore economy. Singapore, which relied extensively on the use of a foreign worker levy to control and manage the inflow of foreign workers to sustain its economic growth, became a focal point of interest in labour-starved Japan and in countries in the Middle East. In the early 1990s, I raised questions about whether the heavy reliance on foreign labour was neces-sarily congruent with maximization of the welfare of the resident population and suggested that Singapore needed a more selective inflow of foreign investment and more moderate growth targets.

Some of the policy recommendations in my later papers included positive discrim-ination in favour of residents (using tax incentives and wage subsidies for employers), the use of administrative measures to compel companies to source for local talent first, the tightening of eligibility rules for employment passes, the lowering of depen-dency ceilings or quotas, and the introduction of minimum wages for lower-skilled foreign workers.

However, the growth maximization stance adopted by policymakers, with eco-nomic growth driven overwhelmingly by employment expansion, continued unabated. This resulted in the size of the foreign labour force quadrupling by 2010 (compared to the 1990s). This in turn led to wage depression, low-wage stagnation, high income inequality, and heightened public displeasure over the overcrowding of public transport and social spaces, the undersupply of public housing, and escalating property prices. It is heartening to note that many of these early recommendations have become part of official policy prescriptions in Singapore in recent years.

The continued presence of low-wage workers whose real incomes have declined over the past decades has resulted in recent research advocating the introduction of a minimum wage in Singapore. I made a strong case to dispel the commonly held view that a minimum wage would result in job losses and higher local unemployment. Instead, with the presence of a large population of foreign workers relative to local workers, a minimum wage would increase the employment of locals, reduce dependence on foreign labour, and raise productivity levels. A significant public debate occurred following the publication of an op-ed on this issue in 2010. In 2012, it was announced that a progressive wage model, which essentially is a *de facto* minimum wage system, would be introduced for some of the low-wage occupations in Singapore.

Developments in the global economy driven by rapid technological change, the prevalence of global value chains, the growing volume of swift international capital flows, the increased migration of labour, and the persistence of informal labour markets have together generated new challenges in labour markets worldwide. Singapore too faces fundamental challenges in the next phase of economic transformation. A 'rising tide that lifts all boats' approach, which has been the main driver and motivation for its economic transformation in the previous four decades, is now widely regarded as unworkable in a society that is marked by unacceptably wide income disparities, persistent transport infrastructure bottlenecks, land scarcity, and steeply escalating housing prices which have adversely affected living standards.

The population paper published in early 2013, which provoked a surge of opposition to a proposed population target of 6.9 million people in 2030, effectively limits employment expansion through immigration as the driver of future growth. Sustaining productivity-led growth through an emphasis on continuing education and skills development and higher wages will instead become the main focus of policy initiatives. Critical to this policy are measures that are directed at improving the productivity of all workers. The constraints of land and infrastructure also necessitate a rethink on the reliance on certain sectors in Singapore's growth strategy. In particular, whether or not the continued reliance on tourism and the creation of high value-added jobs are compatible goals is a question that will need serious analysis.

There is also a need to redirect individual and corporate resources and energies from rent-seeking activities in property to socially-productive investments for long-term national objectives. The potential negative effects of income inequality will require policy reforms that will improve social stability while maintaining or enhancing market efficiency. Due to the increased volatility and unpredictability of employment, there is a need for labour market institutions to provide social protection for the unemployed and temporarily displaced workers. Meeting the basic needs of ageing low-wage, low-educated workers and ensuring the future retirement adequacy of middle-income workers are also essential, and this will require innovative changes in Singapore's social security policies.

The increased uncertainty and vulnerability affecting labour markets as a function of rapid technological change and globalization have become the major concerns of policymakers. Innovative labour policy reforms that have a significant impact on raising or maintaining economic security and living standards are critical. The ground is fertile for more evidence-based labour market policy research in order to produce coherent and efficacious responses to the challenges ahead.

14 The Price of the Invaluable: The Role of Companies and Markets in Water Supply

Olivia JENSEN

"Water" is an easy research topic to communicate. When you tell the person sitting next to you on the aeroplane that you work on water, they nod sagely and say, "Yes, the next world war is going to be fought over water, isn't it?"

Whether or not you agree with that particular claim — I tend not to — there is little doubt that the availability of water is a serious and growing concern for families, farmers, and industries in many parts of the world that sometimes leads to conflict. Within the broad domain of water policy, there are three themes that I work on: the role of private companies, the design and implementation of contracts, and pricing.

Private vs. Public

The issue that drew me into research on water policy was whether private companies should have responsibility for urban water services. As I was setting out on my doctoral research in 2003, the media were full of the controversy surrounding the 'privatization' of water in developing cities, a phenomenon that had spread rapidly in the 1990s. Civil society organizations and unions had staged protests in a number of places; 'water wars' had even been fought in the city of Cochabamba in Bolivia.

In fact, it was not water — the resource — that was being privatized, nor even in most cases the pipes and plants used for the treatment and distribution of drinking water. Instead, private companies were being given the right to manage water supply systems over a period of 20 to 30 years under what is known as a concession contract.

A small handful of European companies had dominated the global market in the 1990s and they stood accused of raising tariffs beyond the reach of the poor, cutting off households that were unable to pay, and at the same time failing to carry out the capital investment that was so badly needed in these systems — and to which they had committed in their contracts — while reaping extraordinary profits.

Two of the largest and most debated contracts in the world had been awarded for the cities of Manila and Jakarta in the late 1990s. In both cities, the French and British companies that had won the contracts had invested less than planned, and improvements in coverage and quality of service had been slow or absent. Why was the experience of private sector involvement in the water sector so different in Indonesia and the Philippines from the UK or France, where the same companies seemed to be providing satisfactory service at a reasonable price?

This was the question I had in mind as I set out on nine months of field research in seven countries around Asia. In each case I collected data about the contract, its implementation, the actors, and the institutional context.

The incentives of the actors and the institutional context are critical factors because long-term concession contracts are necessarily 'incomplete' — it is impossible to describe in the contract every possible state of world that might be realized over 20 years, even less to specify the interests of the parties in those states of the world. This was made resoundingly clear in Asia in 1997–98 when the region was hit by financial crisis and many of the assumptions that were made in the concessionaires' business plans were abruptly overturned. These events set off protracted contract renegotiations during which investment stalled and service levels stagnated.

In an uncertain world, long-term contracts need to strike a balance between flexibility and commitment. They need some kind of adjustment mechanism that allows the parties to respond to changes in the operating environment while circumscribing opportunistic behaviour by either the company or the government. Transparency is also central. A renegotiated contract needs to be perceived as fair by customers and employees if it is to last.

My research has examined several dimensions of contract negotiation, implementation, and renegotiation, and I see much more work to do in this area in the future. I am currently working on a review of PPPs — 'public-private partnerships' — for water supply in Asia using data on contract numbers, types, and the firms involved to show how new forms of private involvement have emerged in the region and how the line between public and private has become heavily blurred. I am also embarking on a study of contract provisions, comparing recent PPP contracts against those of the 1990s. Subsequently, I plan to revisit Manila and other case studies from my doctoral research to see whether the events of the last decade challenge my previous conclusions.

What Makes You Perform?

When I talk about my research on the role of the private sector in water supply, people often ask, "Which is better? Public or private?" It was clear from early on in my PhD that even if you focus on just one dimension of 'better,' say improving access to piped water for poor urban households, the answer is frustratingly equivocal — "It depends."

In some places, publicly owned and managed utilities do an excellent job of delivering services. This will come as no surprise to people who live in Singapore. The surprise is perhaps that so many public water utilities in Asia (and elsewhere) have resoundingly failed to deliver universal access to this basic public service even as national governments have achieved strong macroeconomic growth and robust fiscal positions. PPPs, on the other hand, are clearly no panacea. What are the factors that distinguish high performing utilities, be they public or private?

Part of the answer may lie in the incentives of managers, employees or contractors. Performance-based contracts, in which remuneration is tied to the achievement of certain results, may help to provide these desirable incentives. Contracts of this type are used increasingly widely in the urban water sector in both developed and emerging markets. However, setting performance measures, monitoring, and enforcing these contracts remain problematic.

As I write this, I am beginning a new round of field research, this time in India, to gather data on a particular performance contract, the first city-wide PPP to be implemented in the country. The question of how to improve utility performance may be nowhere more urgent than in India, where no city has continuous tap water supply, coverage is low, particularly amongst the poor, and around half the water supplied by utilities is lost through leaks or pilferage.

I will be collecting data on coverage and quality outcomes and seeking to quantify the impact of the contract on household welfare. The study will focus in particular on increases in the number of piped water connections for individual households and on the relationship between connections and household income and status. While this contract appears to provide balanced incentives to the utility to supply both rich and poor, in practice there may be confounding factors. Yet if this contract does deliver significant improvements, the demonstration effect throughout India could be powerful.

What's it Worth?

People don't seem to have any trouble recognizing the value of water in their lives, and yet if you ask them how much they pay for water, or how much they would be willing to pay, they can rarely answer the question.

Several years ago, as I was mulling over whether to conduct research in this area, I did a quick survey among my old classmates who, conveniently for my purposes, had spread all over the world. How much did they pay for water? Nobody knew the answer offhand. Some dug out their water bills and struggled for a while to decipher them before reporting back that they still didn't know how much they paid for it per litre, gallon, or drum. A few took the trouble to write out the rather lengthy details of their tariff structure for me: so much for the first volume block, more for the second and third, a flat fee for meter rental, an extra charge for wastewater, an environmental tax… It became apparent that even people who receive a detailed bill found it difficult to know how much they actually paid for water.

An invaluable good, universally consumed, without a market price? The paradox of water pricing had piqued my interest. I set out to look at how water is actually priced around the world. Since that first rough and ready survey, I've been involved in a much more extensive and methodologically sound international survey of water tariffs for urban households. A first look at the data show no significant relationship between regional water scarcity and price, for example. There is much more to be done in analysing these data, and this is one of the areas that I am currently working on.

Looking further down the track, I see great potential for research into the pricing of water resources. In the US and Australia, well-established markets for water rights are generating interesting data for analysis. What is more, these markets are being established in Asia. In July 2014, China announced that pilot water rights markets would be set up in seven provinces. How will these markets function in a very different political, economic, and institutional setting?

My work has led me to reflect on the normative question too: How much *should* water cost? Water is at the juncture of social, environmental, and economic spheres. Surely all of these should have a bearing on price, and their weightings will be influenced by the political settlement in any particular community. Yet, I hope that research can inform this debate in ways that help policymakers achieve fair and sustainable outcomes.

Philip Larkin has a poem that begins:

> *If I were called in*
> *To construct a religion*
> *I should make use of water.*

Water may not be quite a religion for those, like me, who are immersed in researching its many facets, but it is certainly an inspiration.

15 From Gangnam Apartments to Urban Development Policy in Asia — A Personal Journey

JOO Yu Min

In the summer of 2003, I was excited at the prospect of going to Harvard University to study for the first time something called "urban planning." To be honest, I was not too sure myself what to expect from a Master in Urban Planning programme; but I knew that I wanted to make a positive difference to how we build and experience our cities. Looking back, I think my interest in cities had gradually developed over time, as I had the privilege to live in three different countries during my childhood and teenage years.

In Korea, I was born in Seoul, in one of the new residential developments of Gangnam, which had begun in the 1970s under the military government's "Plan for South of the Han River." Before then, the Gangnam (translated as "south of the river") was underdeveloped open fields, far from the affluent and trendy urban image that led to Korean singer Psy's famous "Gangnam Style" video four decades later. Once the development had been initiated by the military state, more than 90,000 new apartment units were built in Gangnam within just a decade (1974–1984). They were modern, mass-produced apartment complexes of identical-looking concrete buildings laid out in order, including within the complex a number of residential-service uses, such as playgrounds, small parks, neighbourhood commercial centres, etc. Hence, my early childhood years mostly took place in an urban area surrounded by rapidly rising concrete buildings.

Moving to the suburbs of New Jersey (in the eastern U.S.) was thus a drastic change for me. Besides the fact that I suddenly became a "deaf-mute" at the age of eight — as I knew fewer than ten words in English — it was visually a huge transition as well. My family lived in a single detached dwelling with its own front and back yards, full of immensely tall trees (or so it seemed to an eight-year old city girl). Spiders would hatch their eggs, and cicadas would leave their shells everywhere in the summers. I even remember how one day an eagle dropped from the sky, lying dead on our sidewalk! I felt like we were living in a forest that I only used to read about in children's books.

Paris was another entirely new urban experience for me, compared to an American suburb or a rapidly developing Asian metropolis. Imagine having the cobbled streets, open cafes, street musicians, and romantic old 19th-century buildings as the setting for everyday life! I was a rather bookish high school student at the time, wanting to become just like Mme. Curie (yes, the two-time Nobel Prize-winning female scientist), but Paris nevertheless did not fail to show me how beautiful a city could be. It is true that one had to be careful not to step on dog poo on the sidewalks every now and then, but the city's preservation of the physical characteristics of Haussmann's comprehensive urban renovation of the 19th century was certainly impressive. In addition to Paris, thanks to my energetic dad dragging me all around Europe during summer vacations, I visited numerous European cities with their charming buildings and planning layout as historical legacies.

Thus having been exposed to varied living environments, I began to question why Seoul had so many rows of identical-looking concrete apartment buildings that seemed to literally cover the entire city — something that I had taken as a given before. What Koreans referred to as the "matchbox" apartments (because they look just like standing identical matchboxes row after row) did not seem normal to me anymore. Even the "new towns" developed in the 1990s, with much fanfare of creating the Korean "Garden City" on the outskirts of Seoul, were far from the suburb I had experienced in New Jersey, as they were packed with the same high-rise apartment buildings. So when the Harvard Graduate School of Design asked incoming students to prepare a few photos of their cities to share with other classmates during the orientation, I did not bring in photos of the traditional palaces in Seoul. Instead, I showed photos of the densely built-out high-rise apartment buildings, which I knew to be a key striking feature of the modern city of Seoul. And when people asked me why I wanted to study urban planning, I said (somewhat naively) that it was because I wanted to contribute to transforming Seoul to become a more interesting and attractive city for people to enjoy and live in, besides being a city of colossal apartment complexes.

Of course, even without my contribution, Korea's economic progress led Seoul to gradually move away from building "matchbox" apartments towards more diverse development projects. For example, Seoul's Digital Media City is the world's first high-tech complex with mediated streets, bringing together urban development with digital technologies and wireless communication. The Cheonggye stream project (which received international attention) took down the city centre's 5.84km of deteriorating elevated expressway, in order to restore the stream, giving the public space back to people. Seoul now is increasingly emphasizing the importance of becoming a people-centred and eco-friendly city in its post-industrial stage. While my original goals for the city were partly realized without my help, my quest to find out why the apartment complexes dominate Seoul's urban landscape has nevertheless led to my dissertation, as well as to developing my research insights and interests along the way.

First, I became interested in the multi-level approach to examining urban development and policy. Studying cities can easily be restricted to the local (urban) level, but focusing on the urban level alone did not explain the prolific apartment developments in Seoul. It required an understanding of why and how the Korean national government worked with the private sector to successfully launch the commercialized property market of the new modern apartment complexes, as it attempted to solve Seoul's severe housing shortage while the majority of its funds (the foreign loans) was dedicated to building industries. Seeing a close connection between urban and national development in the Korean experience, I wrote my dissertation on "The City as a National Growth Machine: City-Building and the Role of Urban Development in South Korea's Political and Economic Transitions."

I studied the key urban development projects and policies that generated synergies with industrialization, at varying development stages and institutional settings. Even in researching more contemporary post-industrial and decentralized cities, I find that the multi-scalar analysis of urban development continues to reward the inquirer because cities are increasingly becoming the geographical sites where interscalar relations and competing priorities concentrate and play out in today's global neoliberalism.

Second, having closely followed Korea's urban development along its trajectory of modern economic growth, I value historical explanations in my research. A city's history is not only manifested spatially (as I have seen in many European cities), but is also strongly present in political, institutional, and social institutions and conditions, which impact policy development and outcomes. In other words, cities are not blank slates where policies get developed and implemented — an obvious statement, but sometimes ignored in policy studies. Especially when policy ideas travel very fast and get quickly implemented across national borders amid growing global inter-city networks, historically grounded (and thus more complex) explanations become even more illuminating.

Last, but not least, I have realized that Asian cities do not always conform to the urban theories originated in and based on the West, and so my research interests lie in adding to the knowledge of urban development in Asia. Asia's cities need to find their own models in urban development, as the Asian Tigers have done when they creatively developed urban and economic policies, as well as modified and reinvented policies borrowed from other countries. Asian Tigers' cities, after having achieved economic miracles, should also learn from their own history, and resist mindlessly adopting popular post-industrial urban policies. An accurate understanding of the political economy of Asian cities is important, because it is where the capacity for creative and innovative policy-making can be fostered.

My journey, which had started with the somewhat naïve and limited hope of having a hand in making Seoul a better city, has been recalibrated over the course of studies and research until it has become a passion for advancing knowledge in the field of urban development (focusing in Asia) and for contributing to dialogue with future Asian policymakers on urban challenges, potentials, and policy solutions.

With such a purpose, I now feel privileged to be in Singapore, the stage for some of today's outstanding urban policies; and especially to be at the Lee Kuan Yew School of Public Policy, where the public policy researchers and the future leaders of Asia come together, striving to create a better Asia. Happy 10th anniversary, LKYSPP!

16 Research Passion for Excellence in Teaching

Suzaina KADIR

Excellence in teaching cannot happen without research.

This may seem like a fairly obvious statement but, remarkably, it is not well established. For example, faculty members on the educator/ teaching track are told that their research does not count in their year-end appraisal. Only their teaching scores do. In several faculties, particularly in the hard sciences, research grants are not available to those on the educator track. At best, they are encouraged to apply for smaller grants meant specifically for research that will contribute towards "education theory" or advancements in thinking about pedagogy. Research passions and the attendant products — publications — that lie outside these specific areas are not thought to be important for those on educator track and therefore need not be funded nor considered in the annual appraisal for promotion.

This is odd, given that one cannot teach without research. And one cannot excel at teaching without a passion for research. Let me make three short arguments on why I believe this to be the case.

First of all, course design and content comes with research. The Oxford and Cambridge dictionaries define "research" as "the systematic investigation into and study of materials and sources in order to establish facts and reach new conclusions."[1] Broader definitions of "research" include "the collecting of information about a

---

1   See http://www.oxforddictionaries.com/definition/english/research.

particular subject."[2] Exploring, thinking through, sometimes critically, and gathering information on a subject matter are all essential components when we put together a course and when we design courses, especially new ones.

More than then ten years ago, I was asked to consider designing and teaching a course that would introduce the concept of "gender" to political science majors. The study of gender was just making its way through the university system but had not reached the all-male bastion of political science. I am a woman with a political science PhD, but I had not earned my doctorate in gender studies nor had extensive exposure to the subject matter. But I was interested in the subject and felt a passion for it. I believed strongly that this was an area of study yet undeveloped in the teaching of political science at the National University of Singapore. I agreed to work towards designing a course on "Women, Gender and Politics".

It took me a full six months to design the module. I researched and studied classic texts on gender and politics, women studies, and women's leadership. I extensively researched the sub-topics that I would have to include in a comprehensive syllabus so that undergraduates could get a basic foundation in the subject. I read and reviewed classic books written by Simone de Beauvoir (*The Second Sex*) and Mary Wollstonecraft (*A Vindication of the Rights of Women*), as well as V. Spike Peterson's *Gendered States*, a classic collection on gender in international relations. Extracts from these classic works were then identified for inclusion in the syllabus. I researched other syllabi to get information on how other Schools were teaching similar courses. This included communicating with the faculty who teach these modules in universities in the US and learning from them what should or should not be included in such a course.

After researching and studying the topic over the course of some six months, I was able to put together a well-thought through course titled "Women and Politics in Asia", focusing on the intersection of gender, women, and politics in the Asian context. The course introduced Singaporean undergraduates to the women's movement in the West and how their ideas had reshaped politics and policy in the developed world. It asked students to think critically about how the application of

---

2   See also http://www.merriam-webster.com/dictionary/research.

Western notions of gender and gender equality played out in Asian political contexts. It proved to be one of the most powerful courses I have designed and the most satisfying for me as well as for the students. The student feedback was very good. Many of the then undergraduates who took the course continue to remain in touch with me, and they remember the content and discussions fondly. All of this was only possible as a result of the research that went into the course design.

Secondly, active research drives and adds value to a course in significant ways. It is hard to imagine teaching when the content is not tied to one's research passion. It is possible, as when I had to design a new course from scratch. But I did so with extensive research work in advance. Teaching with a passion comes from teaching one's research passion.

In 2010, I taught a class on political Islam. The content of the course was based on my research work on religious organizations — formal and informal — operating in modern political contexts, particularly in Asia. Students were exposed to traditional Islamic organizations in the Middle East and their transformation in the 21st century. During the course we studied the Muslim Brotherhood and considered the impact and influence of the Muslim Brotherhood in Asia, such as in Indonesia, Malaysia, and Singapore. We explored policy puzzles as governments struggled with different frameworks by which to manage the Muslim Brotherhood and their proxies. We debated what policy options might work in accommodating religious values in the public domain and what struggles this could produce.

My existing research added tremendous value to the content and discussions in class. I was able to present original data sets, and as a class we explored the new information against existing analyses. For example, there has been a tendency to see the Muslim Brotherhood as a geographically-specific organization, operating with a clearly identified structure. My research had pointed to the Muslim Brotherhood as a transnational Islamic movement with cells in Indonesia and Malaysia even though direction still came from Turkey or Egypt. The organizational dynamics within this transnational movement impacted policy options for the movement and its interaction with governments. This is not readily apparent in the understanding of the Muslim Brotherhood at the time.

Discussions in class were vibrant and heated. Students loved it. They poured over original data and discussed the data with me during the class. They questioned some of the findings and helped me refine the research project. My research fed into the content for this course in significant ways. While I could have taught the course without an immediate link to my own research, the research provided additional content that made a big difference to the quality of the class. Students grappled with original data.

In all my years of teaching at the Lee Kuan Yew School, the course on Political Islam garnered the highest student feedback score for me. It enabled me to shine as a teacher and eventually helped me win the Faculty Teaching Excellence Award as well as the NUS-level Faculty Teaching Excellence Award (ATEA). Hence, my third point is that, put simply, original research drives the teacher's passion, and this translates into effective passionate teachers. Former students who took the class still remember it. Many write to me about it. They also helped advertise the course, so much so that when I was unable to offer the class in the following academic year, quite a few students begged to take the course as an independent study module in their fourth semester. Four of them worked with me in a small group. They met with me every week and worked through the syllabus before finally submitting their own research work on a sub-topic related to Islamic political organizations.

For these reasons I am perplexed that research is often cast aside when one is on the educator track for institutions of higher learning in Singapore. At one point, I was told that research did not matter and would not count for those on this track. I was equally horrified to hear that in other faculties, those on the educator tracks were deprived of grants.

To its credit, the Lee Kuan Yew School has always been ahead of the curve in this regard. The School has always valued those on the educator track and not sought to marginalize them. Lecturers, senior lecturers, and associate professors on the educator track have access to internally-generated research grants if they want to apply for it. While they are expected to teach more, they are not penalized for trying to do research.

The University is also moving in the direction of recognizing the importance of research for the career progress of those on the educator track. The Teaching

Academy at NUS recently completed a year-long study with a set of proposals that would formally include research in the assessment of those on the educator track. For example, one of its proposals highlights research as important in the assessment for promotion to the rank of associate professor in the educator track.

The question remains, however, as to what type of research work is important for those on the educator track. The debate over the new proposed structure for the educator track did not touch on what types of research should be recognized. Some were of the view that only research on education should matter. Others protested loudly. For me, one's core research passion is what makes for an excellent educator. This applies to those on the educator track as much as it would for those on the tenure-track. The two — research and teaching — cannot be de-coupled and separated out, and any attempt to do so creates an artificial and unrealistic divide. To insist that those on the educator track only produce research on education when it is not his/her research passion is problematic to start with. An educator's research passions are of great value to his/her teaching, and this needs to be properly acknowledged.

17 Population Ageing in the East and West

KIM Erin Hye-Won

When I began my doctoral studies in public policy at Duke University, I soon discovered how well the field satisfied both my genuine interest in helping disadvantaged people and my academic career goals. The evidence-based approach to improving social policies sparked my interest in programme evaluation and quantitative methods. I became increasingly fascinated by the interplay between government interventions and the family, particularly in the context of population ageing.

My home country South Korea (hereafter Korea) provided an ideal model for my research because its population is ageing rapidly, propelled by extended longevity and low fertility. With its emphasis on economic development, the Korean government tended to minimize its provision of public support for decades, so working-age Koreans bore most of the responsibility for caring for both their elderly parents and their own children. Hence, the erosion of traditional family support for older people is of much concern. My paper with Philip Cook at Duke, published in *Ageing and Society*, documents the continuing importance of children in relieving elder poverty in Korea.

Using data from the 2006 Korean Longitudinal Study of Ageing, we find that almost 70 percent of Koreans aged 65 or more years received financial transfers from children and that the transfers accounted for about a quarter of the average elder's income. While over 60 percent of elders would be poor without private transfers, children's transfers substantially mitigate elder poverty, filling about one quarter of the poverty gap. Furthermore, children's transfers to low-income parents tend to be proportionally larger, so elder income inequality is reduced by the transfers. Over 40 percent of elders lived with a child, and co-residence helped reduce elder poverty. By showing that Korean children still play a crucial role in providing financial old-age security, we demonstrate how important it is for the Korean government to design old-age policies that preserve the incentives for private assistance.

Korea recently introduced various policies to ease the elder-support burdens on families, and the changes have given me rare natural experiments — with implications for countries that are industrializing and expanding their public support programmes — to evaluate the impact of the government actions. The following two projects evaluate the impact of the Basic Old-Age Pension (BOAP), a non-contributory old-age pension, which Korea launched in 2008.

The first project examines how the pension programme affects the likelihood of living alone among unmarried Korean elders. Despite the fact that the living arrangements of older adults impact their well-being, it is not clear whether public transfers for the elderly will increase or decrease independent living. A few natural experiments in the U.S. show such support increases the likelihood that elders will live alone owing to their preferences for privacy. There is no quasi-experimental study in Asia, where multi-generational coresidence is prevalent, and the living arrangement remains normative. I analyzed the 2005, 2007, 2009, and 2011 waves of the Korean Retirement and Income Study (KREIS), a longitudinal survey of nationally-representative Koreans. Overall, the programme has a negative, not positive, impact on the choices of elders on whether to live alone or not. A closer look reveals that the transfers help non-coresident elders to keep living alone and prevent coresident elders from forming one-person households. Ambivalent attitudes towards living alone in a transitional society, together with a modest amount of BOAP benefits, appear to explain the mixed results.

The second project examines the effects of the pension on the life satisfaction of older adults. Despite the keen interest among scholars and policymakers, little is known about whether income affects subjective well-being in later life, a notoriously difficult question to answer, given the empirical challenge of isolating the effect of income from correlated influences and the possibility of reverse causality.

The analysis of the KREIS data provides weak evidence to the effect that the life satisfaction of older adults increases as a result of the pension. These findings on Korea's new pension programme are particularly relevant to other rapidly changing societies where public elder-support systems are expanding and norms of familial elder-support are weakening.

The second broad strand of my research concerns the other major cause of population ageing, low fertility rates, and associated phenomena such as delayed marriage, gender inequality, and labour policy. As the hub of population studies and public policy research in Asia, the National University of Singapore and the Lee Kuan Yew School of Public Policy have provided an ideal environment for my research. While there has been a growing literature on low fertility in developed Western countries, little is known about the phenomenon in the East. It is a question of great interest whether findings from the former apply to the very different contexts in the latter.

Hence, in a project with Philip Morgan at the University of North Carolina at Chapel Hill, we provide up-to-date findings on Korean women's childbearing. Using the 2008, 2010, and 2012 waves of the Korean Longitudinal Survey of Women and Families (KLOWF), we describe whether women planned to have a child in 2008, whether they gave birth between 2008 and 2012, and how the two fertility outcomes are related. Next, we examine what determined the outcomes with logit regressions, focusing on women of parity one. As for determinants, we pay attention to how much husbands and parents help with domestic labour and the use of formal childcare services. Results show fertility intentions are good predictors of fertility behaviour. While both fertility intentions and actual childbearing are remarkably low among women with two or more children, the parity progression of women with one child seems relatively malleable. Gender inequality in the division of domestic labour was striking. When husbands help out, this has a positive impact on fertility intentions. Use of formal childcare affects fertility behaviour positively.

How can one characterize women's attitudes toward marriage and childbearing in countries with low fertility? Although it is well documented that family formation attitudes in general become more liberal over cohorts, little is known about how the attitudes of individuals change over time. More research is needed also on how between-cohort differences and within-individual changes in attitudes relate to important life-stage events, such as marriage, divorce, childbirth, and transitions in education and work. Evidence is particularly lacking in Asian countries. Using the KLOWF data, I fill these gaps in the literature with Adam Ka-Lok Cheung at the Hong Kong Institute of Education. Cross-sectional regression analysis shows younger cohorts are more liberal toward family formation than their older counterparts, which is largely explained by cohorts' differences in experiences of marriage, childbearing, and education. Individual fixed-effects regression analysis reveals that women become more traditional over time and that transitions to marriage and motherhood account for the change.

One common feature of developed Asian countries with low fertility rates is long work hours. Cutting the number of hours people work might contribute to boosting fertility by reducing work-family conflict, but the impact of the number of hours worked on fertility is largely unknown. The Korean government began lowering its legal work-week from 44 to 40 hours in 2004, and this policy gradually expanded from larger to smaller workplaces until 2011. Using this unique policy intervention and analyzing longitudinal data from the Korea Labor and Income Panel Study, with Young Kyung Do and Seoyeon Ahn at Seoul National University, I evaluate whether this change has an effect on the fertility of workers and their spouses as well as on their health and self-reported satisfaction at home and at work.

These findings from Korea have implications for other rapidly changing Asian countries that are following a similar demographic and socio-economic trajectory. Empirical evidence regarding important social policy questions is predominantly from the West, which has a very different context from the East. I will continue to make efforts to fill the gaps in the Asian literature. Recently, I launched a comparative study project between Korea and Thailand with John Knodel at the University of Michigan and Wiraporn Pothisiri at Chulalongkorn University. We examine how differing family systems in the two countries are related to the relative contributions of sons and daughters in supporting elderly parents. In the future, I hope to collaborate more with scholars from various disciplines on comparing countries and examining how their differences shape the interplay between social policy, individual and family behaviours, and well-being.

18 Coincidences or Opportunities?

Ashish LALL

Time present and time past
Are both perhaps present in time future
And time future contained in time past ...

The Four Quartets, T.S. Eliot

Every story needs characters. Mine, to begin with, are my PhD dissertation super-visor, Professor Donald McFetridge, and Alan Jones, a friend, who I will leave for later. We are all deeply influenced by our dissertation supervisors and perhaps owe them a debt we cannot repay. Professor McFetridge is responsible for my interest in competition policy and antitrust. While this is not the main theme of my research, I come back to it every couple of years, and it has led to some very interesting cross-faculty collaborations with my colleagues in Law. It is now also very relevant in the ASEAN region as many member countries are in the process of developing statutes — more than a hundred years after Canada and the United States.

My third character is Professor Richard Brecher, a respected international trade scholar — someone I am sure I disappointed. I was, in my humble opinion, an excellent student of international trade, and Professor Brecher suggested I write a trade thesis. I declined because he was a theorist, and I knew I wanted to write an empirical thesis. However, out of a sense of guilt perhaps, I have written the odd paper about the interaction of trade policy with competition policy and with intellectual property laws.

Alan was a classmate at the time and one semester when we knew that we would have to contend with some very challenging Economics courses, he suggested we look for an easier elective in another faculty. We decided on Transport Economics in the Civil Engineering faculty. Our logic of course was that we probably knew more about economics than engineers and that turned out to be true. An invited speaker from Transport Canada who was duly impressed by our 'intelligent questions' offered us a summer project on productivity and efficiency measurement for Canadian Railways. We gladly accepted although we knew very little about the particular econometric techniques used in efficiency measurement and knew next to nothing about railways. Nonetheless, our work was satisfactory, but the Director at Transport Canada pointed to "some issues with the data".

In the Fall, Alan left for a nice job — at guess where? Transport Canada. I was stuck writing my PhD dissertation on productivity in Canadian Railways...as the Director said, there were "some issues with the data"; clearly someone had to resolve them. Alan's suggestion of searching for an easy course had essentially dictated both my dissertation topic and subsequent research for many years. I worked on the productivity and efficiency of railways and later airports in the United States and also manufacturing industries in Singapore. Although I have moved on to other related areas, I still work on the occasional efficiency measurement project since there are still many unresolved and interesting problems, particularly in aviation.

Later, I moved on to competitiveness, which has less to do with the ubiquitous rankings and everything to do with productivity. In some sense this was a transition from measurement to asking why? And what if anything can we do about it? My earlier work was primarily empirical, so I always had a number, but was not always certain about why the number was what it was. I wrote a competitiveness report for Singapore and later edited a volume on ASEAN countries.

Now I have moved on to innovation, which makes sense, since innovation drives productivity. I focus on information technology because it pervades our lives and its impacts, both good and bad, are only just becoming apparent. I believe this poses some serious questions for all countries although the conversations and debates are taking place primarily in the West. The game is no longer about technology — it's about information. Asian countries need to have serious debates about whether governments are owners or custodians of public data; about freedom of information statutes; about the public's right to know; about privacy and if the notion of privacy needs to be redefined from one based on ownership of data and information to one based on context; about digital identities; and about personal data protection for information collected not just by business but also by government. Public policy in the information age asks societies to re-examine their basic values.

19 Water Narratives: Caricature of a General Theory of Institutional Change

LEONG Ching

So here's the funny thing — in a country that is nearly drowning in rain, why is Singapore so short of water? If you look at the map of the most water-stressed countries in the world, there is only one which lies one degree north of the equator — marked red. That little red dot is Singapore. So that's the puzzle — intrigue always makes a good story.

My work lies in water policies, but my curiosity is stoked by stories. Water stories are the best. Water is essential to life, and so the subject of many political debates. It is too expensive for most governments to supply well, but so cheap that it is often last on the policy agenda. Tragically, it is ubiquitous but so easily polluted — half the freshwater supply in China is undrinkable today.

Three funny stories I've heard recently:

- In Saudi Arabia, oil is cheaper than water (In Singapore, the water bill is one tenth that of the energy bill in a typical household.)
- In Asia, you are warned off drinking from the tap in cities such as Bangkok, Kuala Lumpur, and Hongkong. Yet there is one developing country where

you can drink safely from the tap. That city is Phnom Penh. (Coca-Cola's lab tested it and says it is safe. I tried it for one week and lived to tell the tale.)

- In Hamburg, the average consumption of water is 110 litres a day per person, but in Canada, it is 329. Are people in Canada three times as thirsty?

Stories are the distillation of ideas. They are the sparkles of everyday life. As a writer I am interested in stories, not just as memorable narratives but also as good teachers. The grand name for these lessons and abstractions would be *theories*. Within the many theories informed by water research, I am interested in theories of institutional change.

Institutions are what we usually call "rules of the game" — these can be laws of the land ("Drug trafficking carries the death penalty"), or they can be informal norms ("Drinking (alcohol, not water) is generally frowned upon in the office during office hours"), but what they have in common is that they provide a guide to action.

Water institutions are particularly interesting because they inform two puzzles — development and urbanization. Clean water and sanitation have great impact on the political economy. Drinking water from the tap costs 800 times less than drinking bottled water — having to pay for drinking water is one of the greatest inequalities in developing countries. It is also crucial to public health. A recent United Nations report noted that more than half of the world's hospitals beds are occupied with people suffering from illnesses linked with contaminated water.

More people die as a result of polluted water than are killed by all forms of violence including wars.

Second, cities are the fastest growing centres for human habitation. It is also where water infrastructure can be most efficiently built. Yet, in many cities, water is only delivered for a few hours a day, sometimes not at all for days at a stretch. Governments say they have no money to build the large and expensive infrastructure. But often, significant water savings can result from doing nothing more than fixing leaky pipes and by pricing water correctly. Still, corruption and entrenched powerful interests often connive to subvert these policies.

Added to the bad news is that there is still little consensus on what needs to be done, or even on the magnitude of the problem. Today, in a world of 7 billion people, at least 2 billion people do not have access to clean and safe drinking water (U.N. estimate is 884 million). Equally, there at least 2.5 billion people who do not have access to wastewater disposal and treatment.

Simply discharging wastewater into the seas rather than treating them is especially easy because the oceans are vast. But the cumulative weight of our profligacy means that there is an increasingly number of "dead zones" in the oceans where there is no aquatic life. The largest of these is 70,000, km2 - 100 times the size of Singapore.

The need is great, the solutions obvious, why then is there so little action?

In understanding water reforms (or lack thereof), I use institutional analysis, which is powerful, but in a different way from, say, economic analysis. In economics, the diamond paradox has a very neat solution. Diamonds are pretty useless, or at least less essential to life than water. Why then do they cost so much more? Well, because there are so few of them. Demand and Supply. *Quod erat demonstrandum.*

This sort of conceptual neatness is very hard to find in institutional analysis. Take for example, the simple question: "How do rules change?"

The historical institutionalist will reply — path dependence, historical realities, and they say, things will change but slowly and incrementally — except when they are subjected to external "shocks". But there is something unsatisfactory about a theory which explains things by reference to exogenous variables.

The rational institutionalist does better, by referring to interests. As interests change, so too do rules. But interests are in a constant state of flux — we do not see the same frantic movements in institutions. So, while historical institutionalism explains stasis, rational institutionalism explains change. But neither explains both.

My work in this is to build a theory that accounts for both stasis and change. I argue that this can be done by providing for the role of ideas. An ideational version of institutionalism is not new — my contribution is a small one of quantitatively evaluating narratives. And having done so, to show how particular ideas are embedded within these narratives.

The above is of course a quick caricature, but it is meant to give an idea of the community of scholars who are building a *general* theory of institutional change. This may be vain conceit. General theories are almost impossible to build — even in the physical sciences, we do not (yet) have a general theory of motion — splitting it between Newton for large objects and Einstein for the small. What hope is there for such general theories in social science?

But is that not the nature of research? To make a small chip on a large edifice and hope that in the end the walls of ignorance do come crumbling down? The journey is its own reward.

My journey has taken me from the grasslands of Inner Mongolia to the streets of Jakarta, from the marginal communities in Cambodia to bio-reactor water plants in Singapore. Stories need not confine themselves to geographical areas. Theoretically too, questions of institutional change naturally expand into the realm of learning, cognition, and behavourial science. What, for example, is the role of emotions in narratives? How can I change people's behaviour by changing their minds? How can I test this with experiments?

The questions only end when the journey does.

This essay should end with the answer to the paradox of water in Singapore. It has abundant rain but still is water-stressed — simply because there is no place to *store* the water. Today, some 60 percent of land on the island is water catchment, and the country still imports its water from Malaysia.

But here's the surprise — despite still being one degree north of the equator, despite its small size, despite having far more people, it hopes to be self-sufficient in water by 2030. How? Well, that's another story.

20 Local Government Fiscal Disparities in China

LI Hui

As a public administration and policy scholar, I study public budgeting and finance. The major topics in this field include government spending, taxing, and financing, and in particular, how the government raises revenues to support government programmes — that is, where the money comes from and where the money goes — and the impacts of government taxation and spending on individuals, businesses, and the overall economy.

My primary interest is in the provincial-local fiscal relationship and local government finance in China. More specifically, I focus on the arrangement of fiscal powers and responsibilities across tiers of governments and how those arrangements affect local government fiscal disparities. Fiscal disparities refer to the variation in governments' fiscal capacity, or put more simply, the ease or difficulty with which a local government provides a standard level of public services at a reasonable tax rate or tax burden on residents (Ladd, 1994).

In China, it is widely argued that the efforts over the last twenty years to reform its fiscal policies towards a more decentralized system of taxation and revenue distribution have led to tremendous economic growth. However, there are growing concerns about income and fiscal disparities throughout the country. Evidence shows that income disparities in China accelerated as economic growth became more concentrated in the coastal regions. Some scholars found a sharp rise in either interregional or intraregional fiscal disparities accompanied by a gradual deterioration of public services in underfunded areas. Many have argued that the unsatisfactory income and fiscal distribution may become an increasingly significant obstacle to economic development or political stability.

Although the issue of fiscal disparities in China has been widely discussed, most of the research has focused on the central-provincial fiscal relationship and provincial level fiscal disparities. In general, studies find that provincial-level fiscal disparities remain high after the 1994 tax-assignment reform, but there is debate over whether or not central transfers play an equalization role. There is some work on fiscal disparities across local governments, but fiscal equalization in the provincial-local fiscal relationship is an understudied topic ("local government" here refers to sub-national governments below the provincial level, including prefectural, county, and township governments, but it does not include provincial-level governments).

What remains unclear in the research field is how the fiscal relationship between provincial and local governments has affected local government fiscal disparities. The provincial-local fiscal relationship is an important topic to study because, first of all, current laws and rules do not stipulate fiscal distribution schemes between provincial and local levels. Therefore, provinces vary in how they structure fiscal powers and responsibilities down to their local governments, which will have a critical effect on the fiscal capacities of their local governments.

Secondly, provincial-local transfers, as a second step of intergovernmental transfers, will ultimately decide the effectiveness of the first step — transfers from the central to provincial governments. Without looking at this second step, any analysis of the equalizing effect of intergovernmental transfers would be one-sided.

Thirdly, it is a common practice that local governments in China, especially county-level governments, take the primary responsibility of delivering basic public services to residents, such as primary education, public health, and social welfare. Local government fiscal capacities will obviously affect the quantity and quality of public service delivery in China, which makes the issue of local government fiscal disparities extremely important. All in all, the provincial-local fiscal relationship is an important piece of the puzzle. We need a more comprehensive understanding of the issue of fiscal disparities not only at the provincial level, but also at the local level.

My research seeks to provide a comprehensive understanding of the provincial-local fiscal relationship in China and its fiscal equalizing effects on local governments with a view to developing a sound basis for fiscal equalization policy-making.

First, a comprehensive review of the current status of local government fiscal disparities is essential. While there has been a high volume of provincial-level analysis, my study mainly focuses on county-level analysis, showing how county governments in China vary in their revenue raising capacities to meet their expenditure needs. The research issues associated with fiscal disparities include: How should we measure local governments' fiscal capacities and fiscal disparities? How have fiscal disparities across county governments deteriorated over time? How are provinces different in terms of the variation in their local government fiscal capacities? The results of such inquiry, I hope, will inform China's policymakers when they consider the beneficiaries of fiscal equalization policies.

Secondly, I seek to explore how revenues and expenditure responsibilities are distributed from provincial governments to local governments and how these fiscal arrangements explain fiscal disparities across local governments. Most of the relevant research has focused on central-provincial fiscal arrangements driven by the 1994 tax-assignment reform and fiscal disparities at the provincial level, although a limited amount of analysis is emerging on provincial-local fiscal relationship as well. The key research issues here, in my view, are the following:

- How are provinces different in terms of their arrangements of fiscal powers and responsibilities? In particular, how are they different in sharing revenues with local governments? How are they different in dividing expenditure responsibilities among different tiers of government?
- How would the above differences influence the fiscal disparities amongst local governments?
- How are provincial-local transfer systems designed? How are they different across provinces?
- How well do the differences in provincial-local transfer systems explain variations in local government fiscal capacities? How would this factor interact with the fiscal equalizing effect of the central-provincial transfer system?

A systematic perspective on vertical fiscal relationships across sub-national governments will contribute to this promising sub-national public finance analytical agenda. In particular, research on provincial-local transfer systems and their fiscal effects on local fiscal disparities will fill a void in the literature, most of which has primarily focused on the central-provincial transfer system. On the other hand, little is known about how provincial governments play their role in distributing transfer payments within their jurisdictions and how this would affect the policy effectiveness of the central government's transfer system.

Finally, I seek to give a clear account of current efforts to reform the provincial-local fiscal relationship and hope to make policy recommendations on how to improve these reforms to equalize local government fiscal capacities. Research issues related to the current reforms include: What are the potential paths to take in reforming the current provincial-local fiscal relationship to mitigate fiscal disparities across local governments? What reform efforts have been made so far? What have been the key experiences and what lessons can we learn? What cautionary actions should be taken in further reforms of intergovernmental fiscal relationships? Hopefully the answers to these questions can help sustain the reform effort in China.

Reference

Ladd, Helen F. 1994. "Measuring Disparities in the Fiscal Condition of Local Governments." In *Fiscal Equalization for State and Local Government Finance*, ed. John E. Anderson, 21–53. Westport, CT: Praeger.

21 New Ideas for a 'New Normal' Singapore

Donald LOW

It is commonly said that the 2011 General Election in Singapore marks the beginning of a 'new normal' in Singapore — the emergence of a politically more contested and pluralistic Singapore. According to the conventional wisdom, increased political contestation and democratic pressures will make Singapore less governable, impede quick and enlightened decision-making by government, and increase the likelihood of policies being made for short-term or populist reasons. The underlying message is that given Singapore's unique vulnerabilities, the country is better served by a system of elite governance, guided by the principles that have served Singapore well in the first half-century of independence — meritocracy, the emphasis on growth (over distribution), an emphasis on individual responsibility and an aversion to welfare, and a belief that ordinary democratic arrangements cannot deliver the strong political consensus that Singapore needs to thrive in a turbulent world.

Since joining the School at the end of 2012, much of my research has been focussed on the changing political and policy-making landscape in Singapore, and how this changing context would demand new policy and institutional ideas. One of the main arguments of my research has been how success often sows the seeds of failure. Successful organizations often pursue policies, which were once effective, well beyond their loss point. In Singapore's context, I have argued that many of the ideas that were appropriate, and indeed highly successful, for an earlier context have been elevated to the level of ideology and become "sacred cows" that are not sufficiently questioned or challenged within government.

Take for instance the Singapore economic model. This is a model that is heavily dependent on foreign investments, multinational corporations (MNCs), and a relatively large number of foreign workers and immigrants. It is also a model that prioritizes growth over distribution and one that produces a high level of inequality that the Singapore government, until recently, did not really acknowledge as a problem that merited serious policy action.

The economic model is one of the many things where there is a great deal of consensus within government circles; hardly anyone in government questions it. After all, what choices does Singapore have other than to rely heavily on foreign entrepreneurs and high levels of foreign labour?

But I would argue that the dearth of dissenting voices within government is a recent phenomenon. Singapore's former Deputy Prime Minister, Finance Minister, and the architect of Singapore's economic model, Mr Goh Keng Swee, had this to say about the country's growth model:

> There have been no studies, to my knowledge, of the relative dependence of these countries on foreign investments as an instrument of economic growth. My own subjective impression is that this dependence is strongest in Singapore and that the participation of national entrepreneurs in promoting industrial development is smaller here than in the other countries... Not only is Singapore more dependent on foreign entrepreneurs than are Hong Kong, Taiwan and South Korea, but her position is probably unique in that she is now dependent on a continuing supply of foreign workers to sustain growth... This, then, is the setting against which we have to consider our long-term problem of income distribution... All this involves a fundamental matter of policy. The question we must answer sooner or later is this: 'When do we stop growing?' Or to be more precise, at what point do we stop importing foreign workers and cease to encourage foreign entrepreneurs and capital in Singapore? Because of our limited land area, industrial expansion together with the concomitant population expansion will produce overcrowding to increasingly uncomfortable limits.[1]

---

1   Goh, Keng Swee, *The Practice of Economic Growth* (Singapore: Marshall Cavendish Academic, 1997), p.26.

That Goh Keng Swee was so ready and willing to question not just the country's growth model but also its population strategy in 1972 — seven years after Singapore's independence — suggests that the policy discourse in Singapore has not really advanced. Goh's remarks also hint at the fact that there are more policy options than those presented to Singaporeans, that our economic choices are not as stark and binary as they are made out to be, and that we are better off — as a society and economy — to have a vigorous debate on these issues.

From Hard Truths to Hard Choices

Much of my research on Singapore has been premised on the idea that public policies in Singapore should be guided less by the 'hard truths' that have crept into government over time because of Singapore's success. Rather, policymakers — as well as citizens — are better off thinking about *hard choices* and acknowledging that the principles of governance that have served Singapore well in the first three or four decades are not an adequate guide for the future. The "Singapore Consensus" that tends to dominate any policy discussion in Singapore was also not as uniform and monolithic as we understand it to be today. And whatever consensus we arrive at should be highly contingent and subject to change when circumstances change. As John Maynard Keynes said, "When the facts change, I change my mind. What would you do, sir?"

My work draws heavily on researchers who study why successful organizations find it so hard to adapt to a rapidly changing environment. Clayton Christensen's *The Innovator's Dilemma*[2] and Foster and Kaplan's *Creative Destruction*[3] provide perhaps the most compelling explanations of why successful, previously innovative organizations struggle to deal with disruptive change, why such organizations are better at executing than at experimenting.

To give a concrete example of Christensen's analysis, ask yourself why Sony did not invent the iPod. Sony had created the Walkman, the analogue predecessor to the iPod. As John Kay of the *Financial Times* recounts, Sony was the world's most

---

2   Clayton M. Christensen, *The Innovator's Dilemma* (New York: Harper Business, 2000).

3   Richard N. Foster and Sarah Kaplan, *Creative Destruction: Why Companies that are Built to Last Underperform in the Market, and How to Transform Them* (New York: Doubleday, 2001).

successful consumer electronics company for more than a generation.[4] It had even developed a vision of integration of devices and content long before Apple dreamt of going into the music business. Clearly, Sony was not ignorant about what the future market would look like. And the route Sony followed to create and capture this market was acquisition: it bought CBS records and Columbia Pictures.

So why did Sony fail? Clayton Christensen argues that established companies are naturally resistant to disruptive innovation which threatens their existing capabilities and cannibalizes their existing products. As Kay says, "A collection of all the businesses which might be transformed by disruptive innovation might seem to be a means of assembling the capabilities needed to manage change. In practice, it is a means of gathering together everyone who has an incentive to resist change."[5]

Meanwhile, Foster and Kaplan's *Creative Destruction* points out that successful companies usually suffer from "cultural lock-in". Once a company is successful, it develops deep mental models that consist of its worldviews, beliefs, and the stories that are repeated within these organizations. These mental models are translated into corporate control systems — rules and routines — designed to ensure predictable goal achievement. But these control systems also create *defensive routines* such as the failure to challenge the status quo, the failure to disrupt itself, the failure to encourage sufficient experimentation, and the practice of making failures taboo. In such environments, change becomes very difficult because it requires these organizations to first jettison long-held mental models and practices.

For Christensen and Foster and Kaplan, innovation (as opposed to incremental improvements) rarely comes from existing incumbents, but from new entrants — firms or organizations that are not held back by the mental models, capabilities, and the business models of the incumbents.

Bounded Rationality

Beyond the dynamics of organizational change and inertia, the psychology of decision-makers in successful organizations also helps to explain why they find it

---

4   John Kay, "Why Didn't Sony Invent the iPod?" *Financial Times*, 4 September 2012.

5   Kay, "Why Didn't Sony Invent the iPod?"

so hard to change. Here, the findings of cognitive psychologists and behavioural economists are instructive. At least three of their findings are worth highlighting in the context of a discussion of why change is often difficult for successful incumbents.

First, people generally suffer from an optimism bias that reduces their felt need for change. This bias often manifests itself in the habit of successful leaders spinning their reality in positive ways and ignoring uncomfortable facts. It may also take the form of overconfidence, disaster myopia, confirmation bias, and motivated reasoning.

Second, people are generally loss averse and this makes successful organizations more cautious in exploring and more focused on exploiting their existing capabilities and business models.

Third, the punctuated nature of change — in which a system exhibits long periods of stability before experiencing sudden and abrupt change — tends to reward leaders and managers who are more rigid. A well-known experiment by John Harrington at Johns Hopkins University asked whether organizations with rigid or flexible leaders would do better. The experiment found that the more abrupt and the less frequent the changes were, the more dominant the rigid leaders were, and the worse the organization performed. Flexible managers tended to be promoted in volatile environments, but in environments characterized by punctuated change, they are often marginalized or forced out during the stable periods such that when disruptive change occurs, the organization no longer has such people with the ability to switch tack or change direction.

Thriving in Complexity

A third and final strand of my research has been to apply ideas from complexity science to the study of governance. The essential idea here is that that societies and economies are complex adaptive systems that cannot be engineered, that resilience is a function of our ability to adapt, and that adaptation is an evolutionary process that requires variety, selection, and amplification.

In my recent book, *Hard Choices: Challenging the Singapore Consensus,* I argue that the emphasis on vulnerability in the Singapore government should be replaced by an emphasis on resilience:

> *Resilience — whether of an ecological system, an organisation, the internet, or a species — is a function of two things. First, a resilient system*

is one that has been exposed to a variety of shocks. Each of these shocks is not large enough to destroy the system but over time force the system to adapt and develop diverse capabilities to respond to a wider range of shocks and stimuli. Conversely, systems that are fragile are those that have been insulated from external shocks or protected from competition for long periods.

The second essential ingredient of a resilient system is selection. Resilient systems all have some mechanism for "choosing" between competing, alternative strategies or designs. We normally think of the selection process as being undertaken by individuals or leaders. But selection by distributed, decentralised, and impersonal forces such as market competition is likely to be more reliable in the long run. Markets are resilient because they encourage variety and diversity, and because they provide strong signals for firms to select 'fit' strategies or designs, and then replicate and scale them up. ... It is extremely tempting for the human mind to respond to uncertainty and complexity with a greater desire for control, harmony, and stability. But the reality is that the complete avoidance of shocks and failures is a utopian dream. More problematically, insulation from competition and shocks weakens the signals for the system to adapt, and breeds strategic brittleness and fragility. In the long run, such insulation leads to instability and the system's eventual collapse. This resilience perspective can also be applied to the study of governance. ... A political system can also suffer from too much mimicry, and have too little diversity to allow for the experimentation and adaptation that is needed for long-term survival. Without sufficient diversity, a political system can become trapped by groupthink and ideological rigidity.[6]

Amid rapid global and domestic transformations, I argue that this resilience perspective ought to replace the vulnerability and elite governance frames that Singapore's government has relied on. Rather than emphasize our vulnerability and how it imposes constraints on what Singapore can do or be and why we need to rely on elites, resilience thinking broadens our discussion on governance. It invites us to think about what policy alternatives are available to us, what institutional shock

---

6   Donald Low, *Hard Choices: Challenging the Singapore Consensus* (Singapore: NUS Press, 2014), pp. 7–8.

absorbers we need in a more volatile world, and how we can achieve a better and more equitable allocation of risks between the state and citizens. It also encourages the government to explore how it can tap on the distributed intelligence of citizens, and how democratic practices and institutions can bolster Singaporeans' trust in the government and their confidence in the country's future.

22 Is Humanity Rational?

Kishore MAHBUBANI

I turned 65 in October 2013. At this age, most people retire or slow down. Yet, I find myself working harder than ever. Why? There are many reasons. One big reason is that I am trying to solve a major mystery about the human condition and answer a simple question: is humanity rational?

On the one hand, there is no doubt that on the individual level, more and more human beings are behaving rationally. In contrast to the medieval ages, reason rather than faith drives human behaviour. This is why, as I documented in my latest book, *The Great Convergence*, the human condition is improving by leaps and bounds: conflict is diminishing, absolute poverty is disappearing, and middle classes are exploding. Overall, humanity has never been in better shape. Steven Pinker explains in his book, *The Better Angels of our Nature,* that the reason why human beings are killing each other less and less is because humanity is travelling up an "accelerating escalator of reason that carries us away from impulses that lead to violence."[1]

Yet, on the other hand, while individual human behaviour is becoming more rational, it is not clear that societal human behaviour is becoming more rational. Indeed, there is evidence that the largest and most powerful societies are behaving more and more irrationally, often against their own interests. My goal over the next ten years or so is to try to understand why the world is continuing to experience

---

1   Steven Pinker, *The Better Angels of Our Nature* (Penguin: New York, 2011).

massive examples of irrationality. To demonstrate the nature and extent of the problem, let me discuss three major case studies that deserve deeper examination and reflection.

American Irrationality

The United States of America is by far the most successful society that humanity has produced. It has led the world in many areas over the last hundred years or so. Its list of exceptional accomplishments are far too long to document in a single essay. These include the following: the first (and only) society to send men to the moon; the world's best universities; exceptional entrepreneurship in Silicon Valley; the world's most affluent middle class; the world's freest press and a society dedicated to democracy on the principles of a government "of the people, by the people and for the people."

It is this last achievement that Americans are most proud of. This is why countless American leaders describe America as a "city on the hill", providing a beacon of democracy and human rights that the rest of the world can only admire and hope to emulate. This belief is not based on blind faith. A vast social science industry and a giant media industry reinforce the belief that America has the best government in the world. Leading American minds genuinely believe in American exceptionalism. In his State of the Union Address in 2011,[2] President Barak Obama said that "America is not just a place on a map, but the light to the world."

One of the most astonishing mysteries of our time is the huge gap between American perceptions and American reality. The Americans believe that they have a government that they have chosen and that makes decisions in the interests of the people. Yet this belief is clearly irrational. The reality is that the American government makes decisions that benefit special interest lobbies, not the larger public interest. A few examples will drive the point home.

Firstly, all the polls show that the vast majority of the American people support gun control. Yet the NRA controls the U.S Congress and ensures that even the mildest forms of gun control are killed, even after 20 school children died in the

---

2   Available at http://www.whitehouse.gov/the-press-office/2011/01/25/remarks-president-state-union-address.

Sandy Hook Elementary School shooting in Newton, Connecticut (December 2012) and 12 people were killed while 82 others were shot or wounded in the movie theatre shooting in Aurora, Colorado (July 2012). The social science evidence is clear. Stronger gun control laws lead to fewer incidents of gun-related violence. Yet a small lobby, the NRA, can override the interests and wishes of the American people for stronger gun control laws. Secondly, the polls show that the American people support a balanced two-state solution for Israel and Palestine. This will serve long-term American interests and Israeli interests. Yet as Stephen Walt and John Mearsheimer have documented, larger American and Israeli interests are killed by a small, extremely conservative Israeli lobby. Thirdly, the pharmaceutical lobby (PhRMA), spent US$2.6 billion on lobbying activities from 1998 to 2012 to ensure that the American people would not get the drugs they need but rather the drugs that benefit the pharmaceutical industry.

Fortunately, a well-researched paper documents and proves in detail that the decision-making of the American government is skewed in favour of special interest lobbies, not the interests of the public at large. The paper by Martin Gilens and Benjamin Page states in the conclusion, "In the United States, our findings indicate, the majority does *not* rule — at least in the causal sense of actually determining policy outcomes. When a majority of citizens disagrees with economic elites and/or with organized interests, they generally lose."[3]

Since many of us continue to believe that human beings in advanced and well-educated societies like America make decisions on the basis of reason and logic, it would be natural for the vast majority of the American people to rise up and protest the hijacking of their government by special interest groups. Nothing like this is happening. Instead, despite the evidence to the contrary, the American people continue to delude themselves that they have a government "of the people, by the people and for the people." This incredible capacity for self-delusion is a mystery that I hope to solve through my research.

---

3   Benjamin Page and Martin Gilens, *Testing Theories of American Politics: Elities, Interest Groups and Average Citizens*, 2014: http://www.polisci.northwestern.edu/people/documents/TestingThe-oriesOfAmericanPoliticsFINALforProduction6March2014.pdf.

Chinese Irrationality

One remarkable geopolitical miracle that the Chinese government has been able to pull off is that China has been able to emerge as the number two economic power in the world without disrupting or shaking up the world order. This has been a remarkable feat. In 1980, in PPP terms China's share of the world's GNP was less than ten percent that of the USA and it ranked number 12 in the world. In 2002, it overtook Japan and became the second largest economy of the world in PPP terms, and in a year or two, China will sail pass the United States to become the number one economy in the world in PPP terms.

Having come so far and so fast, it would have been rational for the Chinese government to continue pursuing the same strategy that they carried out in the remarkable thirty-year growth period from 1980 to 2010. In this period, the Chinese government carefully followed Deng Xiaoping's wise advice, captured in twenty-eight Chinese characters, (1) *lengjing guancha* — observe and analyze [developments] calmly; (2) *chenzhuo yingfu* — deal [with changes] patiently and confidently; (3) *wenzhu zhenjiao* — secure [our own] position; (4) *taoguang yanghui* — conceal [our] capabilities and avoid the limelight; (5) *shanyu shouzhuo* — be good at keeping a low profile; (6) *juebu dangtou* — never become a leader; and (7) *yousuo zuowei* — strive to make achievements.[4]

After having done so well for three decades, China has shocked the world by trying to snatch defeat from the jaws of victory. It is clearly irrational to change a winning strategy just as China is about to emerge as number one. But this is what China seems to be doing in recent years. A few examples will illustrate this point. The Chinese government wisely calculated that a strong and cohesive ASEAN community was in China's larger national interest as it provided China with a valuable geo-political buffer against any potential American containment policy, if it ever came about. This is also why China wisely concluded an FTA with ASEAN in 2002. After two decades of successful courtship, China blew it all by vetoing an ASEAN statement at the Phnom Penh ASEAN Ministerial Meeting in July 2012. For the first time in forty-five years, ASEAN failed to agree to a joint communique due

---

4   Kishore Mahbubhani, *The New Asian Hemisphere* (USA: Public Affairs, 2008), p. 224.

to unwise Chinese intervention. In damaging ASEAN unity, China effectively shot itself in the foot. Why did China behave so irrationally?

Similarly, when Malaysia and Vietnam decided to lodge a claim over the continental shelves in the South China Sea in in the UN in May 2009, China reacted unwisely by depositing in the UN a map claiming the South China Sea on the basis of the now infamous nine-dash line. As I document in my book, *The Great Convergence*, the Chinese have metaphorically hoisted an albatross around their necks by trying to defend an indefensible nine-dash line. History tells us that this nine-dash line was drawn by Japanese historians, not Chinese historians. Professor Wang Gungwu, a leading Asian historian, has written that in the 19th and 20th centuries Japanese maps included all of the South China Sea. In 1947, the Nationalist Chinese adopted the map with the Japanese nine-dotted line covering the South China Sea. This map was then inherited by the Communist government, who initially did nothing about it. Today, it is ironic that the Chinese government has to defend a line first drawn by the Japanese and the Kuomintang.

In trying to defend the line, the Chinese government is providing America a geopolitical gift that matches the geopolitical gift that America gave to China by invading Iraq. It is therefore no surprise that American leaders have been second-to-none in declaring that China's leaders are violating international law and the UN Convention on the Law of the Sea (UNCLOS) by drawing the nine-dash line. In a recent speech, the Deputy Assistant Secretary of State, Michael Fuchs, stated that "… a pattern of provocative and unilateral behaviour by China has raised serious concerns about China's intentions and willingness to adhere to international law and standards…the ambiguity of some claims, such as China's nine-dash line, and recent actions in disputed areas heighten regional tensions and inhibit the emergence of cooperative arrangements to jointly manage resources." And the American leaders are able to do this with a straight face even though the United States has itself not ratified UNCLOS. The Americans believe, to use an old American expression, that the Chinese are "leading with the chin" in promoting the nine-dash line, and they cannot not resist the temptation to react to it.

It has not been rational for China to either divide ASEAN or vociferously defend the nine-dash line. If Deng Xiaoping had been around, he would have restrained such behaviour. So the question remains: will China behave more rationally or more irrationally as it emerges and becomes the number one power in the world?

Global Irrationality

In *The Great Convergence,* I have a chapter entitled "Global Irrationality." It documents that at the global level, humanity is making some massively irrational decisions. The main thesis of *The Great Convergence* is that the world has changed fundamentally. In the past, when seven billion people lived in 193 separate countries, it was akin to living in 193 separate boats with a separate captain and crew taking care of each boat. Today, with the world having shrunk as a result of globalization, the seven billion people live, literally and not metaphorically, in 193 separate cabins in the same global boat. The problem with the global boat is that you have a captain and crew taking care of each cabin but no captain or crew taking care of the global boat as a whole.

None of us would sail into a rough ocean on a ship without a captain or crew manning the vessel. Yet, this is what humanity is doing as it sails into the 21st century. We all know that the world will not have a global government in our lifetime. Yet we can and should strengthen institutions of global governance. This would be in the collective self-interest of humanity as a whole. Yet we are doing the exact opposite.

A few examples will illustrate the scale of our folly. On our small, densely connected world, pandemics cross the globe like wildfire. Hence, we have a collective self-interest to strengthen the WHO. Instead, we are weakening it by reducing the predictable, annual financial contributions it receives each year. Similarly, we are obsessed with the dangers of nuclear proliferation. Yet we are financially strangling the one organization equipped to battle nuclear proliferation, namely the IAEA. Thirdly, after the disasters involving two Malaysian aircraft, we need to strengthen multilateral institutions and procedures to protect international airways. Instead, we are doing the opposite.

The big surprise here is that the West is leading the charge in weakening multilateralism. Most Western intellectuals believe that Western civilization is the best educated and most rational civilization on our planet. Yet, in weakening multilateralism, the West is clearly acting against its own long-term interests. So the final question to pose, as I conclude this essay is this: why is the most rational civilization behaving so irrationally?

23 First, Ask the Right Question

NG Kok Hoe

Some five years ago, I embarked on research into the Central Provident Fund (CPF) in Singapore with what I thought was a clear plan. As I was based in London at the time, I came into frequent contact with research on the sustainability of public pension systems among the mature European welfare states. It had been recognized for some time that pay-as-you-go pensions that channel welfare contributions from the working-age population towards pension benefits for contemporaneous retirees would come under increasing fiscal strain as populations age. Much of the pension research at the time was therefore concerned with the capacity of national governments to implement reforms and their impact on wellbeing. Although the CPF is a defined contribution scheme based on individual accounts, it too had undergone some adjustments in response to longer demographic trends. Therefore, I thought it would be worthwhile to model the impact of various CPF reform scenarios on old-age income security.

But as I began to look at the data, I quickly realized that I was on the wrong track. Internationally, the CPF attracts one of the highest rates of contribution — at one point, up to 50 percent of monthly earnings. Yet there is huge uncertainty regarding the amount of pensions it generates in retirement. Simulations of pension outcomes range from as low as 13 percent of individual income to more than 50 percent, depending on one's assumptions about the use of CPF funds, itself a reflection of the extent of individual choice over pre-retirement withdrawals. More importantly, among elderly persons aged 65 and above in the mid-2000s, just one tenth had access to *any* CPF income at all. The *amount* of CPF payouts is therefore a secondary issue to the vast majority of retirees.

As I was used to thinking of the CPF as a pillar of income security in old age, this was unsettling. In reality, family support mattered far more — 80 percent of elderly persons received cash contributions from their children amounting to around two thirds of the parents' individual incomes on average. To focus on CPF reform pathways alone was, to some extent, to ask the wrong question. Instead, I became interested in why a pension system that appears to take so much provides so little. Also, how long can Singapore continue to rely on the prevailing configuration of formal and informal income provision to deliver income security in old age?

Policy Design and Distribution

First, my research considered a number of policy design and delivery issues. As a retirement income system, the CPF does not serve everyone equally. Since CPF savings derive almost entirely from earnings, the ideal individual under this system is one who enjoys an uninterrupted career history, earns a reasonable salary, and makes sensible decisions when purchasing housing using CPF funds. To guard against myopia, a Minimum Sum rule exists to protect a small amount of savings for retirement. But individuals' lives are seldom ideal. Unstable employment or unemployment disrupts the stream of CPF savings. A stable long-term career, but with low earnings, equally translates into a smaller pot of money for retirement. From the perspective of income adequacy, the Minimum Sum merely protects money that is available and does not serve the needs of those who do not have adequate savings in the first place. There is also the issue of gender. Although labour force participation has risen steadily for women in Singapore, it remains lower than men's. Women are also likely to leave the workforce at a younger age, mostly due to care duties at home. This generates a deep gender inequality in terms of financial independence. Elderly women in Singapore have lower incomes and access to far less diverse income sources than men. They depend almost singularly on their children for financial security.

Next, housing is a major factor accounting for the diversion of CPF savings before retirement age. The usual response to this concern is that a home in old age is a considerable financial asset. It means not having to pay rent. It can generate an income stream if spare rooms are sublet, or a one-time payoff if it is traded down for a smaller property. There are also other equity-release schemes such as reverse mortgage through which housing assets can be converted into income. But home ownership should not be regarded as a matter of course even with Singapore's extensive public housing programme. Between 2003 and 2012, out of all the applications for public housing, almost one-tenth were to rent, not to buy (based on Housing and Development Board [various years]). My work on national survey data also found a correlation between individual incomes and home ownership in old age. Persons with lower incomes are less likely to own properties. Housing therefore cannot be expected to reverse poverty or correct inequalities in income distribution among older people.

Even among property owners, the conversion of housing assets into cash income has proven to be more complex than anticipated. Response to the various equity-release schemes has so far been slow. This to some extent is not unique to Singapore. In the United States, some older people keep properties that are larger than they need as a form of precautionary saving. Elderly people in Asian societies may hope to bequeath housing to their children. In Singapore, people may also be confused by mixed messages between the ideal of home ownership as stake-holding, i.e. something identity-defining that should not be easily relinquished, and the notion of homes as financial asset, i.e. something to cash in for monetary gain. In addition, there is uncertainty regarding the value of housing assets at the point of redemption given the volatility of housing prices, particularly if there is a surge in supply due to growing numbers of older people placing their homes on the market.

Then there is an issue of timing. The most straightforward way of estimating pension outcomes is to apply current policy rules to a set of hypothetical income profiles and economic parameters and then calculate the final savings either as a lump sum or annuity. The OECD (2013) takes this approach when assessing pension systems, as does the Ministry of Manpower (Chia and Tsui, 2012). Adopting static policy rules allows researchers to interpret and anticipate the impact of current policy, but does not reflect the experience of any particular individual or cohort. In reality, individuals experience a moving timeframe of historical policy rules with its starting point determined by one's year of birth. For instance, someone born in

1950 and who worked from the ages of 20 to 60 would have experienced the CPF rules from 1970 to 2010, not 2012 rules held in perpetuity. This is all the more important when assessing the CPF due to frequent rule changes over the years, such as adjustments to the contribution rates. Pension projections based on current rules do not represent the policy outcomes for the many generations who are already in old age, or in fact anyone who joined the workforce prior to the year from which the rules are taken. My calculations using historically accurate rules for cohorts entering the workforce between 1990 and 2010 suggest that the effect of recent parametric adjustments to the CPF on income replacement rates may be marginal.

Demography and Sustainability

My research then moved on to examine the larger question of sustainability. As an individual accounts scheme with minimum public subsidy, the fiscal sustainability of the CPF is not in question. The longer-term and more important question is the dependability of family support in the long run and the durability of a system that assigns such a disproportionately large role to informal income provision under conditions of rapid demographic ageing. Whichever indicator we look at — average life expectancy, population median age, or old-age dependency ratio — Singapore is expected to move up the international rankings in the next 20 years. Higher old-age dependency ratios are normally taken to mean less support for elderly parents from adult children at the household level, but there are in fact two countervailing demographic trends at work. Declining fertility directly reduces the number of available children to each parent. Each adult child therefore shoulders a greater share of responsibility for supporting the parents, and adult children will also have to set aside more resources for their own retirement since they are likely to have even fewer children themselves. But with improvements to life expectancy and falling mortality rates, not only do parents live to more advanced ages, the adult children will also have better chances of survival as they, too, age. The impact on family support from the coincidence of declining fertility and improving life expectancies therefore depends on the scale and timing of the two trends.

In Britain, for example, fertility rates surged in the post-war period before entering a phase of decline after the 1960s, whereas life expectancy has been climbing steadily (Murphy and Grundy, 2003). The result is that the proportion of 80 year olds with at least one surviving child will in fact continue to rise for the next 20 years, although the population as a whole is ageing. But in Hong Kong, which has a comparable demographic profile to Singapore, fertility has fallen more sharply and continuously, beyond levels that can be compensated by improvements in the life expectancy of adult children. My own analysis found that the average number of surviving children for mothers reaching the age of 65 in Hong Kong is therefore expected to decrease from 3.4 in 2009 to 1.2 in 2039. This should be worrying for Singapore too, when we consider the role of children in old-age income security.

Given the pace of Singapore's economic development, it may be intuitive to put the income insecurity experienced by current retirees down to historical timing, since they did not enjoy the same levels of income growth and CPF participation as later generations. One-off income and welfare packages targeting current retirees may be attributed to this line of thinking. However, this may be overly optimistic. While CPF savings may grow with successive cohorts of retirees, these will be offset by the loss of income or in-kind services from the family due to the decreasing availability of children. It is the outcome of this trade-off that will determine whether current income arrangements remain fit for purpose. Under certain assumptions, my own projections suggest that elderly persons' likelihood of co-residence with adult children may fall from 72 percent in 2005 to 47 percent by 2030. When older people live with their children, they benefit from income- and cost-sharing with younger, economically productive family members. They also receive care and help with the tasks of daily living. With fewer or no children, not only must elderly people set aside more savings for living costs, they may also have to purchase care services from the market. The prevalence of children's cash contributions too may decline, from 75 percent to 69 percent in the next two decades.

My research in the past few years has led me to think that we need to take the challenge of old-age income security seriously. This is the starting point of a series of evaluative studies I hope to conduct in the coming years into the major domains of social policy in Singapore, beginning with care and housing. The experience has also taught me lessons about policy research. Many social policy problems have a universal character but also take on unique national tones, not least because policy impact often reflects not just policy design and delivery, but also the total configuration of policy decisions, existing social arrangements, and larger forces like demography. Understanding the contrast between national settings makes these configurations more explicit. It also helps with that all-important first step in research — asking the right question.

References

Chia, N. C., & Tsui, A. K. C. (2012). *Adequacy of Singapore's Central Provident Fund Payouts: Income Replacement Rates of Entrant Workers*. Singapore: Department of Economics, National University of Singapore.

Housing and Development Board (HDB). (various years). *HDB Annual Report*. Singapore: HDB.

Murphy, M., & Grundy, E. (2003). Mothers with Living Children and Children with Living Mothers: The Role of Fertility and Mortality in the Period 1911–2050. *Population Trends, 112*, 36–44.

OECD (2013). *Pensions at a Glance, Asia/Pacific 2013*. Paris: OECD.

24 Of Mice and Man: A Personal Research Journey

Tikki PANG

When John Steinbeck published *Of Mice and Men* in 1937 little did he know that the title of his book would one day describe my personal journey in the worlds of scientific research and public policy. Steinbeck's famous tome tells the story of George Milton and Lennie Small, two displaced migrant ranch workers, who move from place to place in search of new job opportunities during the Great Depression in California. My personal research journey similarly describes a search for opportunities which took me from mice to man in order to fulfil my passion for knowledge and its role in improving the human condition.

How did I get to where I am? On reflection it would probably be fair to look at this personal journey as having three distinct phases: the lab rat, the international idealist, and the aspiring policy teacher.

First, the lab rat. Being too weak in mathematics to become an engineer, and too squeamish to ever contemplate becoming a doctor, but with a strong interest in science developed in high school, I enrolled in an undergraduate degree programme in biochemistry where some excellent and inspiring teachers gave me an insight into the life sciences and all its wonders. An interest in life's molecular basis then led to an interest in the newly-emergent field of immunology, which studies how a body responds to, and deals with, attack by external threats, especially microbes. This led me to the pursuit of a PhD to study the immune response to a virus infection in a 'model' system, which involved infecting mice with a virus called mousepox (a distant relative of the infamous smallpox virus) by injecting the virus into the tail vein of the mouse (!). The mice were then sacrificed — black, grey, brown and white mice — and then taking out their blood, spleens, and other organs to perform some exciting experiments in the laboratory. In the course of completing the PhD, I estimated that I had sacrificed around 5,000 mice…

But good things do come to an end and, upon completing the PhD, there was a need to find a job. It was a natural path to enter the academic world where the functions of research, teaching, and service were the norm. Entering an academic institution in a developing country proved to be both an exciting and difficult challenge. The field of immunology was a new one in this part of the world so there was no shortage of exciting research questions to ask, but finding research funding and support for infrastructure was often difficult. However, after 22 productive years pursuing the 'holy grail' of the academic (i.e. 'publications, professorship, patents'), ten of which was spent doing only research, I began to feel a sense of lack of direction, boredom even, and of wondering 'there's got to be more to it than this'. I began to ask questions like "…so you published another 10 papers last year — what does it mean? Is it really contributing to the huge pool of global knowledge? Is it really making a difference to people's lives?"

What I had written and published by that time were largely the outcomes of primary, hypothesis-driven research studies around the immune response to microbial pathogens, as well as studies analysing the molecular nature of these viruses and bacteria. As a result of these contributions to the scientific literature, I began to receive invitations to scientific meetings at the World Health Organization (WHO) to act as an advisor to several committees which were dealing with the challenge of developing new vaccines for preventing diseases afflicting developing countries such as typhoid fever, malaria, and dengue. This opened a completely new world, a world where the focus was not on the *generation* of new scientific knowledge, and publishing for the sake of publishing, but rather on the *use* of such knowledge to improve health outcomes through effective health policies, especially in the developing world. So when a position came up in the WHO to lead a new department called 'research policy and cooperation' I was intrigued and decided to take a leap of faith and leave the security, and the creeping complacency, of the academic world. Being somewhat of a naive idealist, and even a 'left wing' student during my under-graduate years, the idea of working for an international organization with global reach and the potential to improve the health of the underprivileged was a wonderful opportunity which I could not resist.

So enter the second phase, the international idealist. I clearly remember my first day at work at the WHO where I actually had to look up the meaning of the word 'policy'(!). I was given the responsibility, not for *doing* research anymore, but instead to see how research can improve health policy in the member countries of the WHO. This involved working with these countries to improve their capacity to use science to improve the delivery of healthcare, as well as utilizing the WHO's mandate to improve the transparency and accountability of research at the global level. It gave me exposure to what policy is all about at both the national and global levels. After vaguely and gradually understanding what 'policy' means, I discovered that the training I received as a basic scientist served me well, whether I was promoting the better use of evidence in a national policy for selecting a malaria drug, for example, or whether I was developing a global policy to register all ongoing trials for new drugs.

Being a researcher at heart, working as an international civil servant did not diminish my desire and interest to continue publishing and contributing to the scientific literature. I continued to write and publish, though what I wrote were more policy perspectives, 'op eds' and reviews of various sorts rather than primary research articles.

The 13 years spent at the WHO were exciting, exhilarating, and a wonderful learning experience, and widened my horizons beyond anything I could have imagined. Above all else it gave me the privilege of knowing so many global health experts and leaders with their compelling visions and commitment to health improvement, health equity, and social justice. I retired from the WHO with its core mission firmly engraved in my heart: 'the attainment by all peoples of the highest possible level of health'.

While fulfilling and enriching, the work was hectic, sometimes bureaucratic, often political, with exhausting travel schedules. So upon reaching retirement age, the academic within me yearned for the chance to return to an academic environment with time to think, reflect, write and, importantly, pass on the knowledge and experience I gained to others, especially the next generation of young people with the potential to change the world for the better. It was then that I discovered that there were schools of 'public policy', one of which was located in Asia, in Singapore.

So enter the third phase, the aspiring policy teacher. Having left teaching for more than 20 years, and having never taught 'policy', teaching postgraduate courses in a school of public policy was quite a daunting challenge. Will the content be relevant? How will the students react? Will it actually be useful? This third phase is still ongoing and is very much a 'work in progress' where I am constantly learning from a multi-disciplinary and excellent group of colleagues. I have also learned that my students have as much to teach me about public policy as I aspire to teach them about principles, conceptual frameworks, and case studies. I learnt too that my experience in the actual development and implementation of health policies, with all its vagaries and uncertainties, provided a real and practical perspective to the conceptual and academic frameworks of public policy formulation, which the students appreciated.

What are the factors which have driven my research, and how have the various interests in the different dimensions of research evolved, changed, and been translated into a personal research agenda? My research agenda over nearly 40 years can be characterized by an evolution from asking the 'why' question, which characterizes most of basic research, to asking the 'how' question around ways in which knowledge can be used to improve people's lives. It has moved from hypothesis-driven experimental research in the laboratory (e.g. on how we respond to infectious disease) to the laboratory of real life (e.g. on research to improve health care delivery and the governance of global health). In short, it has moved from a focus on 'publications, professorship and patents' to 'people, policy and practice'.

Well, that sort of explains how I got to where I am. Where do I want to go, and how might my research develop in future? I'm not really sure what the answer to that question is, but perhaps a fair response would be "I don't know where I'm going but I'm on my way..." Science has taught me to be an intelligent sceptic, and policy has taught me that science, though necessary, is seldom sufficient, nor is it the only factor in public policy formulation. My research journey through the three phases has also played an important role in the continued development of a research agenda for the future which will centre on the shaping of global health policies and their impacts and a desire to better understand the factors which lead to an effective and cogent interface between the worlds of science and policy where the mind (i.e. the science) and the hearts (i.e. empathic policy which responds to people's needs) meet. As Sir Michael Marmot once stated, "Science does not fall on blank minds which get made up as a result. Science engages with busy minds which have strong views on how things are and ought to be".

I may still be reincarnated as a mouse in my next life, but I hope that my research journey will have had a little impact on improving the lives of men, women, and children especially in underprivileged countries of the developing world. The journey has been characterized by the realization that scientific idealism has to be tempered with the realities of how science is used (or not) in formulating effective public policy, by the importance of minds but also of hearts, and by the desire to help shape the minds of future leaders. My passion for research is undimmed, and the journey continues.

25 Health for All, All for Health — Public Policy Research for Global Health

PHUA Kai Hong

A piece of Chinese calligraphy hanging in my old public health department at the Medical School reads from left to right "*ren ren wei shen*", which in *hanyu pinyin* is roughly translated to mean "the people's health". But if read in the Chinese classical style from right to left, it goes "*shen wei ren ren*" or "life for the people"! So, like balancing the forces of *yin* and *yang*, the relationships between the health of populations and public policies for health can also be juxtaposed in both directions.

Public health is all about life and death in populations, of improving the human condition or maintaining the delicate balance between people and their environments over time and space. It is thus natural for everyone to think, act, and live their lives around health issues, whether for good or for bad. How we eat, sleep, work or play, whether in excess or lack of these functions, will determine our own health in due course and the extent of our longevity. Although we cannot choose our parents or our genes, can we nevertheless attempt to improve our physical and social environments through good public policies and services? As we begin to understand more and more about the social determinants of health and how certain variables can shape our health status or predispose us to certain risk factors, can we not do something about this knowledge and work towards translating the evidence into policy and action? Public health policy concerns people and their governments in caring for their own lives — who, what, where, when, why, and how they live or die. Therein is the reason for my passion in studying public health and in extending public health research into public policy.

Public health policy involves how people value health and of social action towards attaining universal health goals and ideals. The relationships between medicine, economics, politics, and public administration are at the cutting edge of public health. Global public health policy is a relatively new concept that has given rise to a field dedicated to the study of the structures, processes, and activities by which government, multilateral institutions, and civil society actors attempt to position health in public policy and to create new forms of health governance at the global level. Global health governance brings together the disciplines of public health, international affairs, management, law, economics, and the social sciences to focus on activities that shape and control the global policy environment for health. Besides the foreign policy and international trade nuances, the reality is that almost anything that is relevant to the major problems in global health — from improving access to essential drugs and developing vaccines, to managing climate change and environmental challenges that can affect health in vulnerable countries — requires resources that are beyond the scope of individual countries, organizations, or groups.

The Past

Earlier in my life, I had wanted to be a doctor to relieve suffering, cure disease, and save lives. But as an undergraduate at Harvard doing pre-medical studies, I was exposed to an American liberal education requiring me to also study the humanities and social sciences. I studied the social causes of health and disease and was struck by the influence of social determinants, reflecting the relationships between health and development, and the effects of the larger external environment, while recognizing the limitations and potential of medical science, as constrained by health systems and policies. My interests in broader health issues were piqued further at the Harvard School of Public Health, where I was challenged with concerns relating to population growth, fertility, and family planning policies in the developing world. Little did I know that within my academic lifetime I would be researching health issues across the life cycle from birth to death — including the health of migrant populations and emerging infectious diseases, population ageing and the rise of chronic medical conditions, and related social, economic, and other factors in public health and healthcare management.

I left the Ministry of Health and joined the National University of Singapore's Department of Social Medicine and Public Health. When the opportunity arose for me to pursue doctoral studies in public health administration, I chose the London School of Economics and Political Science (LSE), to study under the doyen of health economics, the late Professor Brian Abel-Smith, in the then Department of Social Science and Administration (now renamed the Department of Social Policy). I was fortunate to be exposed to the inter-disciplinary and applied subjects concerned with the analysis of societal responses to social needs and the understanding of theory and evidence drawn from a wide range of the social sciences. Studying social policy gave me the opportunity to reflect on how different societies have developed ways of meeting social needs, or have failed to do so, by relying on informal or family institutions, private markets, or individual actions, or on government action through the welfare state. Social policy enabled me to question the different approaches to social needs and the policy implications from various ideological and disciplinary vantage points.

My PhD thesis was on the development of health services in Singapore and Malaysia, as the two countries in British Malaya had inherited the common colonial legacy of a National Health Service that was centrally planned, provided for, and financed from a dominant taxation system. Part historical and part socio-economic in linking the relationship between social policy and the public health system, my research delved into the origins of the health services and the options for further developing health systems. It became clearer that relevant health policy research would have to translate scientific evidence into public health practices through studies of the political economy of health and of different contexts in any system.

Upon the completion of my PhD studies and as the first fully-trained health economist in Singapore, I was invited to serve on many government health committees — from the Health Advisory Council of the Ministry of Health, to the National Advisory Committee on the Family and Aged (NACFA), and the Government Parliamentary Committee (GPC) Advisory Panel on Health, etc. Thus, I was able to observe at close range and understand the machinery of government policy-making, agenda-setting, advocacy and public education, the complex processes of programme planning, implementation, and evaluation, and to contribute directly from my own research and vice versa.

I was soon appointed the first Adjunct Fellow in the newly-formed Institute of Policy Studies (IPS) to research policy issues relating to the privatization and restructuring of health services in Singapore. My health systems research on reform processes raised policy issues that were not welcomed in certain quarters, although the research was intended to lead to more robust evaluation of government policies and better implementation of health plans. To answer health policy questions more definitively in the future will require greater transparency with respect to data for comparison purposes and even greater accountability in the public provision of health services and the use of public funds. With access to better data, public policymakers will be in a position to spot spurious conclusions or false claims on what has worked or not worked.

The Present

My current research is proceeding along three fronts:

- Health policy, and the development of the Singapore system for innovative healthcare delivery and financing, its regulatory and governance structures
- Comparative health systems research, to analyze best practices and to offer policy lessons in addressing the common challenges of population ageing, integration of health and social care, and public-private participation in health
- Regional health governance, with the objective of strengthening health policies and systems in responding to public health threats, such as infectious disease pandemics, disaster risk reduction and management, migrant health, etc.

My early policy research also coincided with major reforms within the health sector worldwide and locally as the government introduced medical savings and public hospital restructuring. Through comparative health research, we began to compare whether we had indeed built "a better mousetrap" in Singapore's health system, as the world kept beating a path to our doors to learn about our healthcare innovations. A major paradox was why Singapore had spent so little on healthcare but had much better health outcomes than more developed countries.

In a recent publication in *Lancet*, Lincoln Chen and I pointed out that Singapore's excellent track record in health outcomes was more a result of past public health investments in the social determinants of health such as public housing, sanitation, industrial health, education, and economic development through good governance, rather than healthcare reforms such as hospital corporatization and cost-sharing policies. Universal health coverage through the extension of social insurance in Medishield Life constitutes yet another policy response intended to balance equity considerations with sustainability features in the diversified 3-M (Medisave, Medishield, Medifund) system of healthcare financing in Singapore.

In 2010, I was invited to join a prominent regional team to write papers for the *Lancet* series on Southeast Asia and ended up as the co-lead and corresponding author of the overview paper. We took almost a year to review all the current health research publications and to write countless draft versions before publishing our findings in 2011. Through it all, I witnessed upfront the rigorous review process prior to our publication in a world-class journal. I was fortunate to draw upon the experiences of being Principal Investigator of the Asian Trends Monitoring (ATM) project, co-funded by the Rockefeller Foundation and the Lee Kuan Yew School of Public Policy. The ATM horizon-scanning project was linked to ten other international centres of futures thinking that enabled us to share and benchmark our research work. We completed primary research and published 25 issues of the ATM, monitoring trends for regional development, including urban poverty, financial services, education, health, migration, climate change, and food security.

In recent years, I have been co-investigator for two NIHA (NUS Initiative for Improving Health in Asia) research projects: comparative health and population policies in ageing societies of Asia; and comparative public-private participation in Hong Kong, Malaysia, and Singapore. In these projects we studied policy trends and tried to identify best practices and crucial lessons by comparing the policy responses to various challenges. Our research methods and findings found an appreciative audience amongst policymakers, practitioners, and academics around the world. In

2013, we hosted the Social Science and Medicine Conference on Health Systems in Asia at the Lee Kuan Yew School of Public Policy.

Other than the many invitations to present our regional comparative work at international conferences in health policy and gerontology, I was invited to deliver the prestigious S.T. Lee Lectureship in 2012 at the Menzies Centre of Health Policy, University of Sydney and the Australian National University. I also contributed various chapters on comparative Asian health systems and on health and development in emerging economies in authoritative textbooks like the *Routledge Handbook of Global Public Health in Asia* (2014) and the *Oxford Textbook of Global Public Health* (2015). Opportunities are opening up to collaborate further with international colleagues in global public health, including comparing and contrasting the European Union (EU) with ASEAN through comparative health policy and systems research.

The Future

Yet there are currently very few platforms that can bring the many actors together in ways that lead to comprehensive research and innovation for the increasingly complex problems in global health. While there are some successful examples, these represent mostly isolated efforts that cannot be easily replicated to deal with the research and innovation needs in global health. Can we not apply more of the work of experts in global health research and analysis together with policies of governments? How can the research capacity in the universities and think-tanks from the public, private, and people sectors be made available to improve global health systems?

Global health diplomacy is now the new bandwagon, but the complex problems requiring cross-cutting sustainable solutions are also similar at the systems and organizational levels. How do policymakers translate complex science into the art of delivering health services? This requires, among other essentials, greater collaboration and integration at the inter-sectoral, inter-disciplinary, and inter-national levels. Good governance begins with best practices in institution-building at the local and national levels, leading to stronger and more sustainable regional associations like ASEAN, even before global governance. But does ASEAN have the potential and capacity to connect actors and sectors to deliver good health in the region? One of my current research projects attempts to answer precisely this question and to offer possible options to strengthen health governance within a regional system.

The year 2015 is both the 50th anniversary of the founding of modern Singapore and the designated year for the integration of the ASEAN Economic Community. What is in store for the people's health in Singapore and the ASEAN region beyond 2015? The implementation of Medishield Life, as a form of extended social insurance in healthcare financing for the ageing population, signals the start of a new social contract for universal health coverage in Singapore. The issue of who will be covered has seemingly been resolved in favour of the growing numbers of the old and needy. What and how much to provide will have to be balanced by future financing mechanisms and managing the upward pressures of supply and demand in the health care system.

How do we find sustainable and cost-effective ways of providing and paying for healthcare in the growing markets and ageing societies of Asia? Will social care be better integrated with health services to deliver more efficient, responsive, and seamless long-term care for all our chronic conditions and disabilities? Will there be new emerging and re-emerging infectious diseases to test our health systems and governments and our resolve as a society or as a global community? These and many more research questions will continue to keep us busy, as we seek solutions to achieve "Health for All, All for Health"!

26 Bureaucracy, I Love You

Ora-orn POOCHAROEN

I have a love-hate relationship with the bureaucracy and bureaucrats. I grew up having enough food, adequate housing, a good education, and medical care because my mother was in the civil service. I was able to complete all my degrees only because of the generous government scholarships that I received. On the other hand, I also grew up seeing bureaucrats in my mom's office reading life-style magazines and romance novels during office hours. Most would pack their bags and leave for home at 3:30pm when the official office hour ends at 4:00 pm. As adults, we all have experienced bureaucratic inefficiencies, long queues for public services, meaningless paperwork, and demands for bribes. We all have spoken to paper pushers who talk to us like robots — emotionless — and who are always following some invisible standard operating procedure. But hold on, how can I dislike civil servants? I love my mom. Generally bureaucrats must be good people; they are not here to harm us! Thus, with this dilemma in mind, for the last 10 years all of my research projects have had one aim — to understand and find ways to improve the bureaucracy.

In this era of governance, where multiple actors of all sectors are taking ownership of public issues, the role of the bureaucracy and bureaucrats is rapidly changing. Globalization and advance telecommunication technology, together with new expectations of state-society relations, have reshaped the way bureaucracy functions around the world (Poocharoen, 2012). Waves of modern administrative reform, which began in the Anglo-Saxon countries in the 1980s, have reached the shores of many governments. We are all familiar with administrative reform policies such as privatization, corporatization, autonomous organizations, cutting red tape, down-sizing, and performance-based management. Civil servants and public employees who have sacrificed and worked long-hours (or not) to build our nations are now labeled as culprits of the problem. Bureaucracy is on the official list of all economic textbooks for being a source of government failure. By the year 2000, my mother and many of her friends decided to opt for the early retirement package, which means 'thanks for your services but we do not need you anymore'. It was the end of my mother's career (which she was happy about), but it was also the start of my exciting research journey, where I first focused on comparative administration reform.

Many countries' administrative reforms are very political in nature (Boworn-wathana and Poocharoen, 2005). Close observation of these reforms reveals fights to protect turf between politicians and bureaucrats and among key agencies, especially the budget bureaus and the management or human resource agencies (Bowornwathana and Poocharoen, 2010). It is usually through policy transfer via so-called consultants (i.e. academics and professional consultants) that the reform ideas, mechanisms, and instruments are picked up and implemented in a country. While millions of dollars are spent to improve processes such as work flows, total-quality-management practices, ISO certificates, quantification of performance outputs and outcomes, financial systems, and human resource systems, these reform policies are often unseen by citizens. This is unlike normal services such as education, health, and housing. I argue that international standards of transparency and quality of performance information must be agreed upon to monitor and hold international consultants and governments accountable for reform policies the same way we scrutinize other public policies.

Rather than relying solely on consultants, who often provide a one-size-fits all solution, the more we understand each country the better chance we have in getting policies right. For example, in my work on merit systems in Asia, where seven coun-tries were observed, I found that there is no one pattern of policy instruments used to recruit and select new civil servants. Some use entrance exams, while some argue that exams are not meritocratic because it does not holistically measure a person's potential (Poocharoen and Brillantes, 2013). Another example is how governments design their talent management systems for the public sector. This policy, also, does not have one right way. Some governments groom a small group of elites to run the country and see it as a desirable thing to do, while in other countries such policies would be understood as discriminatory (Poocharoen and Lee, 2013).

Regardless of the above different approaches, I argue the bottom line is that the bureaucrats should also be representatives of the people they serve. Thus, selection processes must take into account the background, motivation, and values that potential new hires have. Also, bureaucrats have to strive to create and sustain positive public values for the community. The case of the bureaucracy in the southern-most part of Thailand, which is afflicted by violent sub-national conflict, illustrates this need clearly (Poocharoen, 2010a; Tangsupvattana and Poocharoen, 2009). Surveys show how citizens feel disconnected to certain key public agencies such as the police, the military, and the judiciary (Burke, Tweedie, and Poocharoen, 2013). Ethnic and religious-based sub-national conflicts around the world have similar characteristics. To turn the bureaucracy into part of the solution, rather than of the problem, we need to incorporate the field of public management into these hard political issues and not leave it to political scientists and international relation experts.

In addition to the above, I make two arguments about the field of public management. First, the field needs to move away from being US-centric (Hou, Ni, Poocharoen, Yang, and Zhao, 2011; Poocharoen 2010b). With more and more international comparisons of how bureaucracies and the public sector function in different countries, we are moving closer to building generalizable theories. Comparisons also help to enhance international standards of public services and civil service professionalism. Second, academia should always be connected to practice (Bushouse et al., 2011). By nature, public management is an applied discipline and is taught in professional schools. Thus, we cannot afford to be in ivory towers and talk in the abstract. Public managers need realistic solutions to real problems.

Asia's cases offer a rich mine of information which can help us advance the field. It is a region abundant with interesting and cutting-edge public management innovations. In particular, I like to empirically study the shift of the public management paradigm from traditional bureaucratic control to cross-sectoral collaboration and co-production of services. This innovation of blending policy instruments for both policy design and implementation is an exciting topic. The instruments include public-private partnerships, networks, and alliances. In the course of my research I have learned how bureaucrats creatively work with civil society organizations and the private sector to deliver services in policy areas such as environmental protection, domestic violence, helping special needs children, rehabilitation of ex-inmates, and fighting corruption. The *modus operandi* is horizontal relations of organizations that makeup intricate networks, in which citizens and stakeholders meaningfully participate in the policy process (e.g. Poocharoen and Ting, 2013; Poocharoen and Sovacool, 2012; Poocharoen and Abdullah, 2014). The nature of public participation has changed over the years. It is no longer about getting feedback from citizens, but rather it is a form of power sharing where decisions are made collectively.

In addition to the above, urbanization in Asia is a remarkable phenomenon that deserves close study from the point of view of innovation. In particular, I am studying the governance opportunities and branding strategies of cities (e.g. Poocharoen, Joo, and Heng, 2014). Not only capital cities but also several secondary cities in Southeast Asia are rapidly establishing themselves as new hubs for education, health care, transportation and logistics, and entrepreneurial economies. Local city bureaucracy and bureaucrats are faced with pressures from citizens, national governments, and the international community on many fronts, including disaster management, sanitation management, water and utilities, heritage preservation, education, and basic health services. This drives city administrators to experiment with exciting innovations to get things done — a haven for academics to dive in and study!

In sum, to help the bureaucracy improve and be more effective, transparent, and inclusive, my passion is to enhance our understanding of Asia's public management and city governance. Throughout the years of doing research I have encountered many amazing bureaucrats who work long hours and who fully dedicate their lives to create public value and serve us. They are smart and passionate people (and I am not only referring to my mom!). Unfortunately, most of the time, they are stuck in bureaucratic systems that were designed to serve a different purpose in the past which has not caught up with globalization, technological trends, and changing state-society relations. This is no one's fault, but it is everyone's responsibility to find ways to improve how we do things. Ultimately, that is what governance is all about, isn't it?

So let me end by saying that it has been a wonderful journey studying you and getting to know more about you. I am excited to follow how you evolve and change over the next few decades. And I am more than happy to help you along the way. I love you Bureaucracy!

References

Bowornwathana, B., and Poocharoen, O. (2005). Managing Reforms: The Politics of Organizing Reform Work. *Public Organization Review*, *5*(3), 233–247.

Bowornwathana, B., and Poocharoen, O. (2010). Bureaucratic Politics and Administrative Reform: Why Politics Matters. *Public Organization Review*, *10*(4), 303–321.

Burke A., Tweedie, P., and Poocharoen, O. (2013). *The Contested Corners of Asia: Subnational Conflict and International Assistance: The Case of Southern Thailand*. Consultancy Report. Bangkok: The Asia Foundation. Available at http://asiafoundation.org/resources/pdfs/SouthernThailandCaseStudyFullReport.pdf. Accessed 15 August 2014.

Bushouse, B. K., Jacobson, W. S., Lambright, K. T., Llorens, J. J., Morse, R. S., and Poocharoen, O. (2011). Crossing the Divide: Building Bridges Between Public Administration Practitioners and Scholars. *Journal of Public Administration Research and Theory*, *21*(suppl 1), i99–i112.

Hou, Y., Ni, A. Y., Poocharoen, O., Yang, K., and Zhao, Z. J. (2011). The Case for Public Administration with a Global Perspective. *Journal of Public Administration Research and Theory*, *21*(suppl 1), i45–i51.

Poocharoen, O. (2010a). The Bureaucracy: Problem or Solution to Thailand's Far South Flames? *Contemporary Southeast Asia: A Journal of International and Strategic Affairs*, *32*(2), 184–207.

Poocharoen, O. (2010b). A Personal Memo from a Woman Teaching Public Administration in Asia. In Rosemary O'Leary, David M. Van Slyke, and Soonhee Kim (eds) *The Future of Public Administration, Public Management, and Public Service Around the World: The Minnowbrook Perspective.* Washington D.C.: Georgetown University Press.

Poocharoen, O. (2012). Bureaucracy and the Policy Process. In E. Araral, S. Fritzen, M. Howlett, M. Ramesh, and Wu Xun (eds), *Routledge Handbook of Public Policy.*

Poocharoen, O., and Sovacool, B. K. (2012). Exploring the Challenges of Energy and Resources Network Governance. *Energy Policy*, *42*, 409–418.

Poocharoen, O., and Brillantes, A. (2013). Meritocracy in Asia Pacific Status, Issues, and Challenges. *Review of Public Personnel Administration*, *33*(2), 140–163.

Poocharoen, O., and Lee, C. (2013). Talent Management in the Public Sector: A Comparative Study of Singapore, Malaysia, and Thailand. *Public Management Review*, (ahead-of-print), 1–23.

Poocharoen, O. and Ting, B. (2013). Collaboration, Coproduction, Networks — Convergence of Theories. *Public Management Review,* (ahead-of-print) 1–28. doi:10.1080/14719037 .2013.866479.

Poocharoen, O., Joo Y., and Heng Y. K. (2014). Branding Asia's Capital Cities. Conference paper at the International Political Science Association (IPSA) World Congress 2014, Montreal, Canada.

Poocharoen, O., and Abdullah F. (2014). Controlling or Empowering Non-Profit Organizations?: Dimensions of Accountability in Singapore. In T. Brandsen, W. Trommel, and B. Verschuere (eds.), *Manufacturing Civil Society: Principles, Practices, and Effects.* Palgrave Macmillan.

Tangsupvattana, A., and Poocharoen, O. (2009). *Problems of the Three Southern Border Provinces: Policy Recommendations* (In Thai), Bangkok: Chulalongkorn University Press.

27 Capital Flows, Crises, and Exchange Rate Management in Emerging Asia

Ramkishen S. RAJAN

A decade is a time-frame far too short to evaluate any academic institution. However, despite its relative youth, the Lee Kuan Yew School of Public Policy (LKYSPP) has already made its mark in academic and policy circles. As a research-oriented faculty member, my primary focus is on the research environment in the School and its influence on my own research. I leave it to others to outline the School's remarkable achievements in other areas over the eventful last decade.

I have had the opportunity to visit LKYSPP a number of times over the last decade and have spent close to four years in the School as a visiting faculty-cum-researcher there. I must confess that I have a special fondness for the School as it also helped in refocusing my approach to research and publications.

Until 2005, I had spent my academic career in economics departments. While the critical mass of faculty being narrowly discipline-oriented was certainly beneficial in helping sharpen my research tools and focus, this also in some ways rendered my approach to research somewhat strait-jacketed. By and large, economists look at how they can contribute to the literature by introducing some new theoretical or empirical tools or data sets. The principal aim is a narrow one, namely, to make a marginal contribution to existing work and to be published in well-ranked journals.

There is certainly nothing wrong with this approach, because scientific advancements are more evolutionary than revolutionary.

However, in 2005 when I joined LKYSPP for the first time, I was introduced to a multidisciplinary environment from the start. I found myself having to explain the rationale and importance of my research to non-economists as well as to students who had a voracious appetite for learning about the global economy and were keen on understanding how my research actually contributed to their understanding of it. This helped me to pay greater attention to the bigger picture. What was my research contribution in helping understanding aspects of the global economy, and what policy implications could arise from my research? Posing such questions to myself helped me make a paradigm shift in my research perspective. I was no longer looking at research solely in terms of progress towards tenure and professorship. My stint at the School had got me to critically appraise the value and significance of my research beyond my own immediate and professional goals.

This realization provided the inspiration and impetus for my subsequent research and has helped enhance its overall quality (as evidenced by publication outlets, citations, conference invites, etc). At a school of public policy, I also became more appreciative of the importance of reaching out to the wider community, to disseminate my research findings as well as to engage in policy discussions in a wider perspective. I have consequently been actively engaged in writing op-eds in various major newspapers in Asia, especially in India and Singapore.

As my research expertise is in international macroeconomics and finance, a considerable part of my research and output has been devoted to capital flows as well as exchange rate regimes and policies. Emerging Asia has been the focus of much of my research, which is slanted towards issues and questions of contemporary public policy relevance. My research methodology has involved drawing attention to an economic policy issue of importance, developing an analytical framework to help explore the issues at hand, and devising a simple empirical model to test the hypotheses thus developed. Unlike many of my contemporaries in economics departments who have focused on the modeling per se, and often very complex modeling, I have preferred to use simple analytical and empirical modeling to gain greater insight into public policy issues.

One of the major areas of my research pertains to booms and busts in capital flows and macroeconomic management in Asia. As emerging economies integrate with the global economy and benefit significantly from it, they have also had to face episodes of sudden booms and busts in capital flows. Large-scale capital inflow surges invariably lead to upward pressures on their currencies and domestic liquidity as well as asset price bubbles and inflationary pressures, while sharp capital reversals can lead to currency crises, asset price busts, and serious negative effects on the financial sector and the overall economy. Many economies, in fact, faced such crises in the 1990 and after (Mexico in 1994–95, East Asia in 1997–98, Russia in 1998, Brazil in 1999, Argentina in 2000, Turkey 2001, etc). Crises of this kind can be particularly damaging to emerging economies, with large numbers of people living below the poverty line and with little or no social protection. Many of my papers, books, book chapters, and op-eds have focused on macroeconomic management in a small and open economy that is subject to such booms and busts. These writings can be broadly divided into two areas, as detailed below.

Currency Crisis and Management. One set of my papers has continued to focus on understanding currency crises and financial vulnerabilities and crisis management policies. An interesting policy challenge has been this: why are some currency crises followed by economic contractions while others are not? My co-author, Shen Chung-Hua (National Taiwan University) and I have addressed this issue in a paper published in the *Journal of Economic Integration* (Vol. 21, 2006, pp. 526-550). We specifically investigated two closely-related questions. First, is there a difference in the output effects of a devaluation during "normal" periods as against those during crises periods? After all, during non-crisis periods, real exchange devaluation is seen as an important policy option for promoting exports and output growth. Yet, there has been no attempt in the available literature to make a distinction between crisis and non-crisis periods. We, however, found that the contractionary effects tended to exist only during crisis periods. Building on this, the paper has explored factors that cause a crisis-induced devaluation to be contractionary. This paper has generated significant interest and also won the *Daeyeng Prize* for being the best paper in the *Journal of Economic Integration* in 2007.

In a paper entitled "How Best to Manage New Style Currency Crises?" (*Journal of International Development*, Vol. 19, 2007, pp. 583–606) I argued that the new-style currency crises that have affected a number of developing and emerging economies lately are characterized by "sudden stops" in capital inflows and adverse balance sheet effects. Given the potential high costs of these crises, there is an ongoing debate on how best they could be managed when they do actually arise. This paper argues that the time-honored Swan diagram, appropriately modified, can provide useful insights into how a country might manage a new-style crisis through a combination of policy adjustment and financing. A version of this framework was used by the Office of Regional Economic Integration (OREI) at the Asian Development Bank (ADB) in their presentations to regional policymakers on the policy options and trade-offs when tackling financial crises. (I was a visiting consultant to the OREI-ADB between June 2006 and August 2006 when I worked on this framework.)

In a recent paper published in the *Journal of Macroeconomics* (Vol. 39, 2014, pp. 215–225, with Alice Ouyang of Central University of Finance and Economics, Beijing), we explored the nexus between external debt and export competitiveness. While we found that once external debt exceeds a certain threshold it is negatively associated with export growth, we were interested in determining whether the tipping points varied, based on country characteristics. We tested various hypotheses, including the extent of exchange rate flexibility, the size of foreign exchange reserve holdings, the development of the bond market, the degree of banking sector concentration, and the history of its financial crises.

Monetary and Financial Issues in Asia: Managing Capital Flows. My other set of papers in the broad area of crisis and management has focused more generally on various monetary and financial issues in Asia as countries try to manage their economies in global capital markets. Monetary issues in Asia have become more significant, as the continent holds the largest international reserves in the world and so plays a major role in global macroeconomic imbalances. I have been particularly interested in the consequences of reserve build-ups. Put simply, when a country intervenes in the foreign exchange market to keep the value of its currency low, it has to sell its currency and, in return, accumulates foreign exchange reserves. When it sells its currency, it creates more domestic liquidity which could lead to inflationary consequences unless they are offset otherwise. The extent to which inflationary consequences are offset and the level of success by central banks in Asia in curbing liquidity pressures (the so-called "monetary sterilization") have been the focus of a series of papers which I have co-authored with Alice Ouyang and Tom Willett (Claremont). Among the most significant of these is a paper entitled "China as a Reserve Sink" published in *Journal of International Money and Finance* (Vol. 29, 2010, pp. 951–972). In this rather well-cited paper (the working paper version of which has been in circulation since 2008), we note that China has been stockpiling international reserves at an extremely rapid pace since the late 1990s and has surpassed Japan to become the largest reserve holder in the world. The paper — an empirical investigation to assess the extent of *de facto* sterilization and capital mobility using monthly data between mid 1999 and late 2005 — finds that China has been able to successfully sterilize most of these reserve increases, thus making it a reserve sink, as Germany was under the Bretton Woods system. Recursive estimation of offset coefficients, however, finds evidence of increasing mobile capital flows that may undercut China's ability to continue high levels of sterilization.

Other related areas of interest have been exchange rate management and trying to understand the types of exchange rate regimes in Asia and strategies pursued by regional policymakers. While many economies claim to have moved to flexible regimes, evidence suggests that they continue to intervene extensively in the foreign exchange market. In a series of papers, Tony Cavoli of the University of South Australia and I have attempted to gauge the extent of exchange rate flexibility in Asia, the types of inflation targeting regimes operated by many Asian emerging economies (Korea, Indonesia, Thailand and the Philippines), and other issues. A book by us — *Exchange Rate Regimes and Macroeconomic Management in Asia*, Hong Kong University Press, 2009 — is devoted to issues related to exchange rate and monetary policy and financial integration in Asia.

My paper with Victor Pontines (Asian Development Bank Institute, Tokyo) in *Economic Letters* (Vol. 111, 2011, pp. 252–55) shows that many emerging economies want some sort of exchange rate management with a stronger bias towards preventing appreciations than towards depreciations. In other words, while it is commonly believed that many emerging economies in Asia are best characterized as having "a fear of floating", we maintain that Asian exchange rate regimes in the 2000s could be more precisely described as having a "fear of appreciation". The results we have arrived at confirm the existence of an asymmetry in central bank foreign exchange intervention responses to currency appreciations versus depreciations in all six economies. This asymmetric exchange rate intervention explains both the relative exchange rate stability and the sustained reserve accumulation in emerging Asia, making the oft-noted "fixed versus flexible" debate about post-Asian crisis exchange rate regimes appear misguided and rather simplistic.

Journal publications and authored/co-authored books apart, I also co-edited the two volume Princeton Encyclopedia of the World Economy (2009) with Ken Reinert (George Mason University) (I was in charge of the International Finance section) and have published various books in the field with major university and commercial publishers as well.[1]

Overall, I have remained extremely research active and been working on issues relating to: financial liberalization, macroeconomic management in emerging Asia, outward investments for emerging Asia, economic re-balancing in China, exchange rate management, and issues relating to competitiveness in emerging Asia, to name just a few areas/topics. I hope that my association with LKYSPP in the next decade will be as productive and fulfilling as the previous one.

---

1   See http://ramkishenrajan.gmu.edu/publications/books-and-monographs/.

28 Destiny, Detachment, and Public Policy

M RAMESH

All sentient beings are adhered to Karma, depend on Karma and take rebirths according to their Karma....Beings are heir to Kamma.

Gautama Buddha

Therefore, without attachment, do thou always perform action which should be done; for, by performing action without attachment man reaches the Supreme.

Krishna to Arjuna, in the *Bhagvad Gita*

I was born in Bhojpur, Bihar, one of the poorest and most hopeless places on the planet. It is not too far from Lumbini, where Buddha was born, and close to Gaya, where he attained enlightenment. Patna, from where Asoka ruled his vast empire and set new standards of good governance, is where I went to school. Studying problems of destitution, sickness, old age, and how to address them through public policy and governance has been with me since birth, I feel.

Having beaten the odds of a dismal child mortality rate, my mother wanted me to be a doctor. I rather liked the idea too because I fondly remembered my village clinic where they gave away red and green syrup in pretty little bottles. But without the opportunity or aptitude for studying medicine, I studied literature and politics. Little did I know at the time that I was destined to be a doctor nevertheless.

Uncertain about what I wanted to do for a career, I stumbled into enrolling in a doctoral programme in Political Science in Canada. I don't know why I chose to write my dissertation on the Canadian shoe industry, but it made for lively conversations and a quick doctorate. Soon, I was in a position to write "Dr." before my name. My mother was pleased.

However, my journey to becoming a doctor was only half complete. Another decade would pass before I would begin diagnosing policy problems and prescribing solutions. I spent the ensuing years reflecting and writing on politics, political economy, and theories of public policy that together formed, in retrospect, an excellent preparation for studying public policy.

My doctoral dissertation on the Canadian shoe industry did not find much favour with publishers, but it did land me a casual teaching position in Canadian political economy at Simon Fraser University. Lecture notes prepared for the course led to the publication of a co-authored monograph *The Political Economy of Canada* in 1992. The book was favourably reviewed and widely used, leading to the publication of a second edition in 1999.

Formal study of public policy was a matter of pure chance. While in the Department of Political Science at National University of Singapore (NUS), my first full-time teaching position, the Head asked me to teach two courses in Public Policy. Protestations that I knew almost nothing about public policy made no difference to the assignment, beyond his assurance that I'd do fine. So I taught and learnt, in that order, about public policy. Within a few years, I had co-authored a textbook on Public Policy (*Studying Public Policy*, Oxford University Press, 1995) which turned out to be a bestseller of sorts, translated into several languages and used at dozens of universities around the world. I was moving closer to my destiny, unknown to me.

My journey took another turn after I met Mukul Asher, who was in the Department of Economics at NUS at the time. In a casual conversation, he suggested I consider shifting my research to some uncrowded new area, such as social policy in Asia. He then gave me a carton of documents on pension reforms in Asia to read. I was hooked. By sheer coincidence, the Head of Political Science at about the same time advised me to stay away from studying Singapore, for my own good. What it was about Singapore that he did not want me to find out, I do not know, but I am glad I ignored his advice. Within a few years, I had published several articles in reputed journals (including *Asian Survey, Journal of Commonwealth and Comparative Politics, Governance,* and *Social Policy and Administration*). I then headed down south to New Zealand and subsequently to Australia, where they paid me less but did not tell me what not to study or write.

The shift in my geographic focus of study from North America to East and Southeast Asia was propitious, as it gave me a front seat on remarkable innovations in social policy. What happened in other regions over a period of decades often occurred in the region in a matter of years, even months, which was opportune for someone arriving so late to the study of social policy. There were not only a lot of new things to write about, there was also a massive appetite for publications on the region, from which I benefitted tremendously.

Then the Asian financial crisis struck in late 1997, wreaking havoc on households and communities in the region. Eruption of the crisis was followed by an unprecedented level of interest in social policies in the region, which inexorably drew attention to my publications that would have otherwise gone unnoticed. I had been writing about the need to strengthen social protection in the region without much effect, and it all suddenly seemed so mainstream amidst the crisis. A boost to my career was one of the few good things that came out of the crisis. I increased my writings on social policy in Asia, resulting in the publication of two authored monographs *Welfare Capitalism in Southeast Asia* (Macmillan, 2000) and *Social Policy in East and Southeast Asia* (Routledge, 2004).

My move to the Public Policy Programme at NUS in 2002 and the opportunity to work with colleagues from different disciplinary backgrounds, all committed to addressing public problems, sharpened my policy orientation. Working with colleagues with formal training in Public Policy, which I did not have, deepened my appreciation for the need to not just analyze public problems but also find solutions to them. Researchers trained in Political Science and other social sciences often do not sufficiently appreciate the need for problem solving, restricting their scholarship to highlighting the history and sources of public policy challenges. There was so much more to learn about studying public policy than I had realized.

My appointment as Professor of Social Policy at the University of Hong Kong in 2008 added a new dimension to my research. Working with colleagues with a background in Social Work, I came to realize that social policy was not just about what governments did but also how governments and policies affected people. I developed an empathy for those whose social protection and health care I wrote about that was missing from my earlier works.

I hope that the greater policy orientation and heightened sensitivity to the human impact of policies is evident in my recent work on health policy published in journals such as *Health Policy and Planning, Development and Change, Social Science and Medicine*, and *American Review of Public Administration*. I am pursuing the same orientation in my ongoing research on social protection in a range of countries in Asia.

Along with delving into social policy in Asia, I have begun to focus more on broader issues of governance and its effects on public policy. This follows the realization that at the root of many public problems lie poor institutional design and weak governance capabilities. I am fortunate to have colleagues at the LKY School who are full of comradery, good ideas, and difficult questions. Discussions of what governments should and can do have mixed enjoyably with Friday evening merriment.

Recently, I have begun comparing the political economy of development in China, India, and Indonesia. I have had a promising start, with articles on China and Indonesia appearing in reputed journals. For the first time, I am formally studying India, and I ask myself if the experience of growing up in Bihar is an advantage or disadvantage.

In the coming years, I will continue to study social policy within the broader public policy and governance contexts, bearing in mind Buddha's caution and Krishna's counsel.

29 My "Research Passion" — Securing the Survival and Well-Being of Our Species

John RICHARDSON

My research passion has to do with questions of sustainability, in this instance the sustainability of the human species on our planet, which I believe is threatened. What is the challenge of "sustainability" that our species faces? Lee Kuan Yew School students learning system dynamics modeling get in touch with this by creating a simple computer simulation of a deer population living on a grasslands ecosystem. When a policy intervention eliminates mountain-lion predators, the deer population overshoots the carrying capacity of its habitat and collapses. As the scenario ends, there is a new equilibrium. A small number of malnourished deer populate a once verdant environmental niche that has become a wasteland.

Of course the circumstances facing our human species are more complex than this simple example my students experience, though the principles are similar. Human beings are both more inventive and profligate than deer. Planet earth provides not only food, but also the resources that energize human society and sumps that receive our wastes. However, the issue of sustainability is the same: is the carrying capacity of an ecological niche sufficient to sustain a profligate population in dynamic equilibrium? Some economists argue that human ingenuity can expand our planet's carrying capacity infinitely, that, in contrast to the circumstances of the deer population, growth need never end. Global models have been created to help resolve that issue.

Global Modeling

A controversial book, *The Limits to Growth* (1972), coauthored by the late Donella Meadows and colleagues, posed carrying capacity issues facing the human species in a new and compelling manner. Like my students, the authors crafted a system dynamics model. It was the second of a new genre of policy analysis tools, the *Global Model* (Jay Forrester's *World Dynamics* model was the first). Model-generated scenarios raised the possibility of an overshoot and collapse scenario, severely impacting the sustainability of the human species, which might occur sometime after the mid-21st century. The quality of the model, combined with aggressive promotion by its sponsoring organization, The Club of Rome, catalyzed a high-profile debate about how much growth in population, capital accumulation, resource consumption, and waste generation was sustainable.

Recent compilations by the Club of Rome, on the occasion of the book's 40th anniversary, point to sales of over 12 million copies and translations into 37 languages. Two successor volumes, *Beyond the Limits* (1992) and *Limits to Growth: The 30 Year Update* (2004), have also received wide distribution. The model has exhibited amazing durability. The essential message has remained unchanged. Sustainability of the human species requires that we live within the carrying capacity of our planet.

Publication — and promotion — of *The Limits to Growth*'s message evoked a new research endeavour, "Global Modeling," using approaches that competed with system dynamics. The competing projects used various theories and computer simulation techniques to examine issues relating to sustainability of the human species that *The Limits to Growth* had raised. For example, my own global modeling work contributed a multi-regional food and agriculture sub-model for the multiregional global model described in the book, *Mankind at the Turning Point* (1974), co-authored by M.D. Mesarovic and Eduard Pestel. It sought to answer the question, "Is the specter of starvation impacting the human species caused by physical limits of our planet's capacity to produce food?" The answer was "no". People were hungry because they were poor.

Of much greater consequence for me, personally, was co-authorship (with Donella Meadows and Gerhart Bruckmann), of *Groping in the Dark: The First*

Decade of Global Modeling (1983). This was the first of several books, making the results of sustainability-focused public policy research widely accessible, that I particularly enjoyed writing. It began as a conference proceeding — of the Sixth International Institute for Applied Systems Analysis (IIASA) global modeling conference — but evolved into something quite different.

Three qualities made *Groping in the Dark* distinctive. First was its *format*. It began with a parable and ended with a prayer. Four different colours of paper distinguished the book's four distinctive themes. It included cartoons and personal reflections of the authors, some expressed in blank-verse poetry. A *theme of consensus* was its second distinctive quality. *Groping in the Dark* highlighted areas of agreement regarding the future of the human species among seven groups of high-profile academics from different disciplines, each passionate advocates of their own global model and critics of competitors. This differed radically from the popular media image of squabbling prima donnas presenting differing views of humanity's future who could not agree on anything. Given its deviation from academic norms, the book's *academic credentials* were also distinctive. Representatives of IIASA's National Member Organizations, including the US National Academy of Sciences, the British Royal Society, and the USSR Academy of Sciences, refereed it. John Wiley and Sons, one of the world's leading publishers of books in the sciences, technology, and engineering published it.

The most widely quoted excerpt from *Groping in the Dark* was twelve "lessons about the world" on which the seven global modeling projects agreed. Here are three of the most important ones.

- *There is no known physical or technical reason why basic needs cannot be supplied for all the world's people into the foreseeable future. These needs are not being met now because of social political structures, values, norms and worldviews, not because of absolute physical scarcities.*
- *Population and physical capital cannot grow forever on a finite planet.*
- *Cooperative approaches turn out to be more beneficial in the long run to all parties than competitive approaches.*

Our current situation is not hopeless, we concluded. *It is challenging.*

Two Non-Academic Books that Issues Raised
by Global Modeling Evoked

Two books that elaborated issues raised by global modeling work quickly followed. *Making it Happen: A Positive Guide to the Future* (1982) sought to make the Club of Rome's messages about sustainability more accessible to Americans. "Americans are natural futurists," the book emphasized, "The American experience has been an American experiment." Ursula Meese, the wife of President Reagan's friend and confidante, Attorney General Edwin Meese, thought enough of *Making it Happen* to gift a copy to the President when they joined the Reagans for a Camp David weekend. I never heard whether it made any impression.

Ending Hunger: An Idea Whose Time Has Come (1985) was the product of a collaborative project catalyzed by *Limits to Growth* principal author Donella Meadows. The book's "author" was the sponsoring organization, The Hunger Project. In collaboration with a gifted writer and inspired teacher of writing, Dr. Elizabeth Neeld, I wrote much of the book's final draft, culminating a four-year project. Like *Groping in the Dark* and *Making it Happen, Ending Hunger's* message was empowerment: "Hunger exists. It doesn't need to. People can make the difference in making the end of hunger an idea whose time has come." The book sold nearly 100,000 copies and, via an "Ending Hunger Briefing," given by Hunger Project volunteers, reached thousands more.

Learning about Conflict, Development and Terrorism
from Sri Lanka's Civil Wars

There can come a time in the life of a professional academic when life becomes too easy. I knew this was happening when repetitions of my "messages from global modeling" to new audiences were warmly welcomed, but required little in the way of new creative insights. When one becomes conscious of this, it is time for a change.

In my case, a concern that had nagged at my conscience for years provided the motivation. "Did my global-modeling-related work for Iran's Imperial Government contribute to the scenario that transformed the country from modernizing autocracy to an Islamic Republic?" I asked myself. More generally, I queried, was it possible, or even probable, that international development practice could contribute more to deadly conflict than enhanced well-being.

Seeking an answer to this question — the answer was "yes" — set me on an improbable journey of more than twenty years' duration. While my research questions now differed from those engendered by public policy problems in the areas of my previous work — urban development, water resource management, and sustainability — my practice, system dynamics modeling, remained the same. New "events data" indicators of violent conflict and state sanctioned violence, appropriate to the long time horizons that system dynamics modeling requires, had to be created. Databases for the three countries on which I focused, Argentina and Mexico (covering the period 1900–1980) and Sri Lanka (covering the period 1948–1988), had to be compiled. When the application of my first model of conflict-development linkages failed to reproduce historical data for the divergent conflict/state sanctioned violence patterns of Argentina and Mexico, fundamental revisions were required.

My initial research design envisioned a ten-country study, adding eight additional cases to the work on Argentina and Mexico described in a 1987 *Futures* article, "Violence and Repression: Neglected Factors in Development Planning." What ultimately emerged, but not until 2005, was an in-depth study of a single case, *Paradise Poisoned: Learning About Conflict, Terrorism and Development from Sri Lanka's Civil Wars.* This was followed by a series of eight small, inexpensively priced, volumes, four in Sinhala and four in Tamil, comprising excerpts from *Paradise Poisoned*, with the series title, *Lessons from the War.* When circumstances in Sri Lanka permit, I am hopeful that six to eight additional volumes will be forthcoming.

Lessons from *Paradise Poisoned* have informed public policy in both the US and Sri Lanka. However, as would be expected for a topic such as this, those processes have mostly been low profile and "off the record." Perhaps the most important single recommendation, from among ten with which *Paradise Poisoned* concludes is this: "Meeting the needs and aspirations of fighting-age young men should be the first priority of national development policies and programs funded by international donors. That the segment of society with the greatest power to disrupt should also be among the most disadvantaged seems paradoxical. The potential consequences of failing to change these policies are perilous."

Singapore: A Land of Opportunity for System Dynamics Modeling

I should at this point allude to my current research agenda, focused on Singapore. As with *Paradise Poisoned,* this has exemplified the principle of moving out of my comfort zone, while continuing to ground my research in system dynamics modeling practice. In a recent journal article, "The Past is Prologue: Reflections on 40 Plus Years of System dynamics Modeling Practice" (2013) and one forthcoming, "Taking on the Big Issues and Climbing the Mountains Ahead" (2014), I have described the exceptionally warm welcome accorded me by the Lee Kuan Yew School of Public Policy and the inspiration provided by the original, evocative writings of Dean Kishore Mahbubani. I have described how Lee Kuan Yew School professors K.E. Seetharam and Gopi Rethinaraj welcomed my collaboration in their teaching of system dynamics modeling. I have described the enthusiasm with which Lee Kuan Yew School students and those from other NUS departments have embraced the practice of system dynamics modeling and produced outstanding projects, based on original modeling work, in the course of a single semester.

In *The Past is Prologue,* I highlighted three attributes that make Singapore a land of opportunity when it comes to the skillful application of systems thinking, especially when it is rigorously grounded in system dynamics models intended to contribute to the shaping of public policy. First is the degree to which Singapore's political-social economy has been shaped by the systems thinking of its founding political leaders, especially Lee Kuan Yew and Goh Keng Swee. Second is the typical profile of Singapore's top leaders, especially those who occupy the all-important Ministerial and Permanent Secretary positions. Most have educations that combine degrees in science, technology, and engineering, with additional graduate work in public management. Third is the strong emphasis on science and technology in Singapore's secondary schools. This makes Singapore an unusually receptive environment for achieving system dynamics modeling creator J.W. Forrester's goal of a society populated by "systems citizens." I believe this goal is attainable, in Singapore, in my lifetime. An NUS initiative, in which I have been asked to play a role, namely, the creation of a residential college with a systems thinking/systems analysis theme, can provide an important catalytic impetus towards attaining this goal.

Looking to the Future

Though Singapore offers a promising and not yet fully exploited venue for system dynamics, I believe initiatives I have sketched, focusing on Singapore, are far too limited. Challenges threatening the sustainability of the human race demand a more ambitious agenda. The problems of potential global system overshoot and collapse to which the *Limits to Growth* model and other global models first called attention, are now far more pressing. Prestigious scientific organizations whose leaders once derided the warnings sounded by global modelers now echo them. There is an important role to be played in Singapore — the promoting of a culture of public policy decision-making that incorporates systems thinking, modeling, and analysis to an even greater degree than presently. However, the opportunities extend far beyond Singapore's borders: to nations that look to Singapore for viable, innovative models of public policy practice and development.

The most important of these, of course, is China. I first become conscious of the opportunity that China offers to system dynamics from Dean Mahbubani's speeches and writings. It is unusual to have two books fundamentally transform one's worldview. For me, Dean Mahbubani's two most recent books, *The New Asian Hemisphere* (2008) and *The Great Convergence* (2013) produced such a transformation. Though my optimism about probable futures is more guarded, Mahbubani's descriptions of China's emergence as a world power and his contrasting of China's economic policies and governance strategies with those of the United States opened new vistas for me.

I believe that many in China are open to new visions of how regional, national, and global economies function. I believe they are open to new visions of development that include sustainability, carrying capacity, and resilience as values. The challenge is this: Can our community of those schooled in system dynamics communicate a powerful, compelling body of both theory and practice that will capture these leaders' thinking? More important, can we catalyze the education of a generation of students with the capacity to communicate and manifest that body of theory and practice more widely? Personally, I am optimistic. A most important source of my optimism is the transformation that students in my classes, especially brilliant students from mainland China, have experienced from applying system dynamics modeling practice to the creation of their own models.

What of my own future research agenda? Using system dynamics modeling and focusing on Singapore, initially, I am seeking answers to the following questions: "How should we deal with the limits of the Earth to build a truly happy society without making society and the economy unstable?" And "What indicators should we use to measure society's true progress and happiness?" These questions top the agenda of Japan's Institute for Studies in Happiness, Economy and Society (ISHES). ISHES was recently founded by Japan's "first lady of the environment" and one of my most inspiring role models, Junko Edahiro.

Envisioning a Future Role for System Dynamics Modeling in Asia

I do not use the term "envisioning" casually. Envisioning became a powerful tool I internalized from a workshop entitled *Leadership and Mastery*, led by Peter Senge and Robert Fritz, that I attended many years ago. The workshop's message, attributed to Walt Disney was this: "If you can dream it, you can do it." Senge and Fritz added the phrase "Vision is a source of power and mastery." I have realized that many of my research projects, along with the articles and books that chronicle them, have been guided by the power of envisioning.

In March 2012, I celebrated my 74th birthday in Singapore. I had just finished reading Ezra Vogel's brilliant biography of Deng Xiaoping (2011). I learned that the year Deng became paramount leader of China was also the year he celebrated his 74th birthday.

I wrote a note to myself and pasted it below the keyboard on my MacBook Pro. It remains there today.

> *Deng Xiaoping was born in 1904.*
> *He became paramount leader in 1978.*
> *He led China through October 1992.*
> *His leadership transformed the country.*
> *What I have done is preparation for what I will do.*
> *My most productive years lie ahead.*

30 The Big Picture and the Small, the Long View and the Short

Razeen SALLY

We shall not cease from exploration
And the end of all our exploring
Will be to arrive where we started
And know the place for the first time.

Little Gidding, T. S. Eliot

I suppose I can trace my research interests back to the day I acquired political consciousness. That was at the age of six — the result of vicissitude rather than precocity. On that day, the Sri Lankan CID barged into the family home unannounced, turned it upside down, and took my father away. Six years of tribulation followed. He was a victim of turbulent Sri Lankan politics.

That direct, personal impact of politics sparked an obsessive interest in current affairs, local and international. It led me, over a decade later, to undergraduate and graduate degrees at the LSE. I read economics and politics. For my graduate work, I specialised in what was then the relatively new area of international political economy. My PhD topic — multinational enterprises and industrial policy in Germany and France — allowed me to spend much of that period in those two countries; indeed, I found myself in West Germany when the Berlin Wall came crashing down. I honed my French and German; and, well, got to know some of the natives, which is usually the best part of "field work". Thankfully, I tired of my conventionally narrow PhD topic only towards the end of the process. I wouldn't dream of re-reading my thesis, and only recommend it to my worst enemies.

My scholarly preoccupation in the 1990s was the history of economic ideas — known fondly to its practitioners as the "wrong ideas of dead white men". I climbed from the narrow gullies of a PhD topic to the Olympian heights and panoramic vistas of Great Thinkers and their ideas down the ages. It was breathtaking and totally absorbing. Joseph Schumpeter, one of the twentieth century's truly great economists and perhaps its greatest historian of economic ideas, said that an appreciation of intellectual history — how ideas germinate, and how they unfold and mutate — gives one a much better appreciation of economic policy, past and present. That rang true for me.

I immersed myself in the pantheon — Hume, Smith, Ricardo, Mill, Marx, Schumpeter, Hayek, Keynes. I savoured the thoughts of their interpreters — Schumpeter, Lord Robbins and Jacob Viner in particular — not only for their content but also for their particular literary and intellectual styles. It was around this time that my own world-view was settling into a classical-liberal mould, in the spirit of the Scottish Enlightenment of Hume and Smith and, fast-forwarding to the twentieth century, of Hayek and Friedman.

Along the way I familiarised myself with German thinkers associated with the Freiburg School and "social market economy". These were economists, lawyers, and the occasional sociologist, most of them linked to Ludwig Erhard, the architect of the post-war West German Economic Miracle. They had a distinctively German philosophical heritage, and they were forged by the crises and ultimate apocalypse that befell Germany in the first half of the twentieth century. They were and remain hardly known outside the German-speaking world — unlike the Austrian economics that travelled the world via Mises and Hayek. But I found unmistakeable connections between this German tradition and the wider, overwhelmingly Anglo-Saxon, classical-liberal canon.

All these strands led to my first post-PhD book, *Classical Liberalism and International Economic Order.* Here I lined up several thinkers — Hume, Smith,

Knight, Viner, the afore-mentioned Germans (especially the economist and sociologist Wilhelm Roepke) and Hayek — and looked at what they had to say on questions of international economic order. I tried to sum it up in a rounded classical-liberal view of global economic policy today.

By the late nineties I was ready to get my hands dirty with policy analysis; the big picture of intellectual history was no longer enough. The area I chose — trade policy — was not directly related to my PhD topic. But I had got acquainted with it earlier, through the history of ideas, and from co-teaching a graduate course on trade policy. First I got stuck into WTO matters — when hell broke loose at the WTO Ministerial Conference in Seattle in 1999, and in the run-up to and launch of the Doha Round in late 2001. Then I followed the twists and turns of the Doha Round as it crept to a halt. This was also the time of a new wave of free trade agreements (FTAs). These had spread earlier in Europe and the Americas, but, from the early 2000s, they proliferated in Asia and other parts of the world. So I turned my attention to FTAs as well, especially in Asia.

Part of the benefit of applied policy analysis, if done properly, is that it gets the researcher out of the ivory tower to mix with real-world practitioners — policy-makers, businesspeople, and union and NGO representatives. That is what I did with gusto. For the best part of a year I ran the trade-policy programme of the Commonwealth Business Council in London, organizing seminars and one big government-business summit. I became active in free-market, free-trade think tanks such as the Institute of Economic Affairs in London and the Cato Institute in Washington DC. I started going to Asia for trade-policy research and consultancy; I worked on trade issues in China, India, and the ASEAN countries. Hong Kong and Singapore became my Asian bases for a few months of the year.

In 2006, I co-founded the European Centre for International Political Economy (ECIPE), a think-tank specialising in EU trade issues in Brussels. I became a regular Eurostar traveller between Brussels and London. Brussels rapidly became one of my least favourite towns. It is slovenly by European standards, with dysfunctional public services — a bit of southern Europe stuck incongruously in the heart of northern Europe, reflecting the history of Belgium. The locals, the Bruxellois, are a parochial lot. Its EU quarter is soulless. Its public statuary seems to be designed by official committees. And it is peopled by Eurocrats and hangers-on who obsess about arcane EU procedures. The real world seems a planet away.

My work on trade policy tries to combine two thrusts. One is "objective" analysis; the other is normative, when I wear my free-market, free-trade beliefs on my sleeve. The audience I have in mind is a mix of experts, policymakers, and intelligent readers and listeners with a general interest in international trade: a broad audience, in other words, meeting at a junction of academia, think tanks, and policy practice. That appeals to me much more than intramural conversations within narrow academic specializations. My book on trade policy, *Trade Policy, New Century: The WTO, FTAs and Asia Rising*, has this kind of pitch.

And now to the present. Singapore and the Lee Kuan Yew School have been home for the past two-and-a-half years. I live in Asia and visit Europe, not *vice versa*. Having spent a decade-and-a-half on trade-policy details, taking in the small picture and the short view, I find myself looking for the big picture and the long view again. I am thinking of writing a book on "Asia in the world economy" — big picture indeed. This will be based on the elective I teach, of the same title, at the LKY School. In it, I cover East and South Asia, from Japan, South Korea and Taiwan to China, Hong Kong, the ASEAN countries and the Indian sub-continent. And I cover three global economic-policy issues: macroeconomics and finance, trade and investment, and energy and environment. Such a book would demand a substantial, multi-year effort.

Just in the past two years I have got acquainted with a new subject: cities and their competitiveness. I did not choose the subject deliberately; rather it happened adventitiously. I have just completed a year chairing the World Economic Forum's Global Agenda Council on Competitiveness; city competitiveness was our big project, for which I coordinated a WEF report, complete with thirty-three city case studies. I wrote the case study on Singapore as a "global city". The experience has whetted my appetite to go deeper. Perhaps a book on what I consider to be the world's five truly global cities: London, New York, Dubai, Hong Kong and Singapore. But that is still an inchoate idea.

One of these days I hope to return to the scholarly pursuit that has animated me most — the history of economic ideas. I would like to teach a course on it again. And get back to writing about it, but perhaps after a few more seasons of age and experience. As Jacob Viner said about this *metier*, "unlike golf, it improves with age."

Last, but far from least, middle age finds me trying my hand at writing of a very different, non-academic sort. I am almost done writing a book on Sri Lanka — an "everything book" containing history, current affairs, a little family history, a lot of travelogue, and other things besides. I have long wanted to do this kind of writing — travel writing in particular. Not exactly an academic's "research passion". But enormously stimulating and enormous fun. And addictive.

31 The Professorial Life: Seamlessness, Synergy, and Significance

Kenneth Paul TAN

I've always believed that the best kind of professor takes research, teaching, and service seriously. At a time when the worldwide landscape of higher education is becoming increasingly dominated by research-intensive universities competing on sometimes very narrow sets of criteria to rise up the global university rankings, it will take the courageous efforts of a cadre of passionate and well-balanced professors to defend the nobler qualities of academic life against such pathologies.

Some universities, of course, are secure enough to rise above grotesquely reductive compulsions. But most are not generally immune from the tendency to limit what is regarded as valuable in academic practice to the efficient and copious production of research outputs with little or no respect for originality and impact on both the academic and professional fields as well as the world that we all live in. And all of this is usually achieved at the expense of good quality teaching and service. As it turns out, it is often the professors themselves who become all too cynical about their vocation and choose to reinforce what is harmful about it by feeling and acting like victims of a system that tends to reduce intellectual creativity and drive to mere machinery and output in a highly audited workspace. In such a culture, newer faculty, sometimes ill-advised, develop perverse anxiety that stands in the way of intellectual joy, discovery, experimentation, and courage to say more than just what is already obvious, widely accepted, and easily citable.

In the last fourteen years of my career as an academic in the National University of Singapore (NUS), of which the last seven years have been spent at the Lee Kuan Yew School of Public Policy, I have considered myself fortunate to have the opportunity to work in a highly ranked research-intensive university, where a balanced approach to the professorial life is possible as long as quality is demonstrated on all fronts. In such an environment, professors can regain focus on their authentically creative role in producing and disseminating valuable knowledge, and providing the leadership to facilitate the individual and collective dimensions of this activity. That is to say, they can reclaim their essential roles as researchers, educators, and leaders. In this essay, I suggest that research, teaching, and service can be a seamless fabric in the professorial life; and, beyond that, they can complement one another in synergistic ways that create the conditions of possibility for significant contributions. Through this lens, I reflect on the strengths and limitations of my own academic practice.

The Research-Teaching-Service Nexus

If I were today asked what my research is about, I would very easily describe it as a critical, qualitative, and interpretive analysis of the tensions that emerge from Singapore's transition from a developmental state to a neoliberal global city, explored through various interconnected dimensions such as creative city policies (including the urban development, arts, media, and education sectors), evolving practices of governance (including public engagement and public morality), notions of liberalization (economic, cultural, social, and political), and issues of justice (through the categories of class, race, gender, and sexuality).

But when I look back over the years, it is clear to me that this research programme is a convergence of quite disparate trajectories since the time of my doctoral work in social and political sciences at Cambridge University. Mostly, this has been the result of my having approached the three pillars of the professorial life — research, teaching, and service — not in a compartmentalized way, but as thoroughly connected and interdependent activities. Each provides energy, inspiration, and resources; opens up new opportunities; and sets new directions for the others, sometimes in fluid and unexpected ways, at other times as a result of strategic calculations.

Bringing Research into Teaching, and Teaching into Research

I was able to build a strong foundation in teaching in the early years of my academic career that began in 2000, when I joined the NUS University Scholars Programme (USP), then a new cutting-edge liberal arts programme with an abiding interest in interdisciplinary curricula, innovative pedagogies, and digital cultures. Without compromising on research activity, my colleagues and I took our teaching very seriously and derived great professional satisfaction from experimenting with active learning approaches, whilst casting a firm eye on the actual achievement of learning outcomes. In 2009, after having won numerous teaching prizes, I was awarded the Outstanding Educator Award, the most prestigious honour given by the university to recognize teaching. I firmly believe that being able to bring my own research into the classroom has been a key factor in my effectiveness as an educator. These days, I'm inclined to approach my teaching in a "research-like" way, taking it beyond the intuitive level.

In many ways, I have also allowed my teaching agenda and goals to shape the direction of my research. In the early years at USP, I designed and taught political science modules, making extensive use of films and other multimedia resources for vividly illustrating abstract theories, concepts, and perspectives. Before too long, I got interested in thinking and writing critically about the arts and popular culture as important sites of social and political contestation and negotiation in Singapore. I started presenting conference papers and writing journal articles and book chapters on media representations and stereotypes, censorship policies and practices, and contested representations of national identity. Much of this work culminated in a scholarly book *Cinema and Television in Singapore: Resistance in One Dimension* (Brill, 2008) containing chapters on the economics and politics of sitcoms, drama serials, and the *Singapore Idol* series on television, and the commercial, art-house, and politically challenging work of filmmakers Jack Neo, Eric Khoo, and Royston Tan respectively.

Not surprisingly, the backbone of my work has always been in mainstream political science and public administration. I have published on Singapore's electoral, party, and parliamentary systems, grassroots democracy, and pragmatism and meritocracy as principles of governance in Singapore. In fact, my 2008 article "Meritocracy and Elitism in a Global City: Ideological Shifts in Singapore" (*International Political Science Review*, 2008) was among the first to offer a systematic, theoretically sophisticated, and critical account of Singapore's evolving practice and conceptualization of meritocracy, which have since commanded much attention from scholars, government officials, and the general public.

I have also allowed my political science and public administration work to branch out of this backbone and connect with my teaching interests in gender and sexuality. I have, for instance, published articles on the emasculation and feminization of Singapore's civil society by a patriarchal authoritarian state. I have also connected my political science work with media and gender studies, for example in the article "Pontianaks, Ghosts, and the Possessed: Female Monstrosity and National Anxiety in Singapore Cinema" (*Asian Studies Review*, 2010). One book project that I am currently working on, tentatively titled "Contemporary Patriarchy in a Global City", is a synthesis of my work in politics, administration, gender, and media.

In 2001, while at the USP, a colleague and I designed and taught a module on the theory and practice of civil society. Our students engaged with theories and case studies in the classroom to make sense of experiences that they gained during semester-long practical attachments to civil society organizations. At the same time, assignments and classroom activities were designed to encourage students to challenge the theories through their practical experiences. Without realizing it, we had introduced "service learning", a well-established educational practice in the US, to Singapore at a time when the language of active citizenship was gaining traction in an apparently liberalizing polity. Several years later, I published an article "Service Learning Outside the US: Initial Experiences in Singapore's Higher Education" (*PS — Political Science & Politics*, 2009), which analyzed comparatively the emergence of service learning in both countries. This and some earlier articles that reflected on my own pedagogical innovations have formed the basis of work on higher education that I am now doing in the emerging field of the Scholarship of Teaching and Learning (SoTL).

Bringing Service into Research, and Research into Service

My interests in cinema and the arts extend beyond the boundaries of academia. In 2003, the socially conscious theatre company The Necessary Stage (TNS) commissioned me to compose music for *Revelations*, its avant-garde entry at the Singapore Arts Festival that year. Immediately after that, I was invited to serve on its board of directors, which I have done until today. In this capacity, I developed an interest in the political power of theatre and, in 2013, published one of my most important articles, a piece on Forum Theatre, which is an audience-interactive practice that had been introduced to Singapore by TNS in 1993 and was almost immediately proscribed by the government from 1994 to 2004. My article, titled "Forum Theater in Singapore: Resistance, Containment, and Commodification in an Advanced Industrial Society" (*positions: asia critique*, 2013), explores the political and economic dimensions of this de facto ban and subsequent legitimization and popularization of the practice in Singapore today. While my service to Singapore's theatre scene has contributed to my own research productivity, I have also been able to apply my research skills to the work of the theatre company. In 2012, I urged TNS to create a full digital archive of annotated recordings of its performances over the years and other related materials, and to make them available as a multimedia online resource. I am now actively supervising this massive project.

Since 2005, I have been the founding Chair of the Asian Film Archive's Board of Directors. The archive's mission is to "save, explore, and share the art of Asian cinema". With a collection of almost 2,000 films from the region, the archive runs an extensive outreach programme consisting mainly of public screenings, conferences, forums, and workshops. Without a doubt, my involvement in the archive has contributed to my Singapore cinema and television book as well as the many articles and chapters I have published on Singapore cinema. I am now bringing my research into my service contributions by editing a book of scholarly essays to commemorate the archive's 10th anniversary.

From 2012 to 2013, at the invitation of Minister Heng Swee Keat, I served on the committee of Our Singapore Conversation, a year-long national-level public envisioning exercise. I was able to contribute to the process by drawing on my research expertise in public engagement and the various dynamics within Singapore's public discourse, including the ideological and political polarizations that have been widely observed. I was also able to obtain ethnographic observations and fresh insights in order to generate new publications, including a number of opinion editorials that appeal to the general public, as well as materials that are especially useful for executive teaching. All of this new writing expands and refocuses my earlier work on the impact on governance and policy-making of moral panics, religious and secular reasoning in the public sphere, and the social divisions that are often ideologically constructed around a liberal and conservative binary.

My emerging research project on Asian creative cities has benefited from these three service commitments to community and nation, particularly in studying the creative economy and creative governance in Singapore.

Within NUS, I have never refused administrative and leadership responsibilities. As a young Assistant Professor entering his fourth year, I was appointed Assistant Head of the Political Science Department. When I moved to the LKY School after my seventh year, I was appointed Assistant Dean. Today, I carry a very heavy administrative load as Vice Dean for Academic Affairs. One of my responsibilities has been to consolidate, codify, and implement a major redesign of the School's curriculum. Beyond the LKY School, I have been a Fellow of the NUS Teaching Academy since its founding in 2009 and was elected to serve as Chair of its Executive Council from 2012–2014. I have written about the role of Teaching Academies from a public management perspective. As a Fellow, I enrolled in a six-month course on Leadership in SoTL offered by the University of British Columbia, working on a project to evaluate the effectiveness and impact of the LKY School's redesigned curriculum. While this research project helps me do my job as Vice Dean, I also expect a few SoTL publications to emerge from it.

Significance

My research projects and outputs have been broad-ranging, interdisciplinary, and sometimes a little quirky. Even though nearly all my work can be understood within the coherent framework of Singapore's transition from developmental state to global city, I am aware that my work is vulnerable to the criticism that it could lack focus and depth. Thus, I have been very careful to ensure that very nearly all of my publications have been single authored and that my research is placed in high-quality peer reviewed publications. In this, I have been fortunate to be able to publish in so-called "tier-1 journals" in both the social sciences as well as the humanities.

However, I am also very mindful that, as someone who publishes single-authored work on Singapore, within the conventions of different academic fields, and often in interdisciplinary ways, my citation figures, especially the H-Index, will never rise to stratospheric levels. Thankfully, this does not trouble me. Allowing my research — and indeed my academic decisions more generally — to be led by intellectual curiosity, emerging interests, creativity, a sense of usefulness, and rich experiences in teaching and service, all the while staying excited about writing and publishing, makes the professorial life so much more fulfilling and enjoyable.

32 The Need for a Serious Rethink on Economics

Dodo J. THAMPAPILLAI

The perception that something is quite wrong with economics has surfaced recently with a fair degree of vigour. For example, the *Economist* (16 July 2009) carried a lead article titled "What Went Wrong with Economics". This query was followed by several critiques of economics — all of course centred on the global financial crisis. To name a few, Nobel Laureate Stiglitz (2011)[1] questions the validity of standard economic models and their imperfections whilst the Australian icon Quiggin (2013)[2] notes the preoccupation with issues associated with the Phillips Curve since its advent in 1958. I believe that these greats and many others, who have reasoned about the failure of economics, have failed to grasp the fundamental source of the problem.

Something is amiss in economics at a foundational level. Economics is firmly centred on the principles of *self-interest* and *present aims*. Given this centre of gravity for economics, social stewardship and altruism remain exogenous to the economic model — not endogenous within the model. The basic model is of course that of perfect competition. Economists argue that self-interest and present aims within the confines of perfect competition would lead to socially desirable outcomes. However, human

---

1   J.A. Stiglitz, "Rethinking Macroeconomics: What Went Wrong and How to Fix It", *Global Policy*, 2(2):165–175, 2011.

2   J. Quiggin, "The State of Macroeconomics: It all Went Wrong in 1958", *e-axes*, December 2013.

history is more a chronicle of conquests, conflicts, failures, and crises rather than a narrative of socially desirable outcomes. Note that the first financial crisis on record was in 1637 (Tulip Mania in Holland) — well before Adam Smith (1776)[3] suggested the possibility of perfect competition as a concept. The analytic formalization of the theory of perfect competition was commenced by Edgeworth (1881)[4] and subsequently completed by Knight (1921)[5]. This formalization however did not instil sufficient safeguards that could avert undesirable outcomes such as those of the Tulip Mania.

In this essay, I wish to argue that the inadequacy of the basic model of perfect competition is responsible, at least in part, for the succession of failures that societies have endured to date. Note that just within one decade (2000–2010) there were at least eight major crises in the world without counting the issues pertaining to climate change. My thesis is that the theory of perfect competition must be modified or rather extended to include sustainability as an explicit condition. As argued below, the role of altruism and stewardship, which are indeed the norm of various religious teachings, are central to the attainment of sustainability.

Economists of different religious persuasions — all of which have similar moral and ethical premises — have been reluctant to inculcate such premises within economics. Hence I present next two fables that I grew up with in Northern Sri Lanka (Jaffna). These fables — one from the Hindu tradition and the other from the Christian tradition[6] — are narratives of altruism. I then proceed to suggest that the morals of these fables can find their way into the body of economics if the conditions of perfect competition are extended to include the sustainability of nature (and hence society).

The Fables and Altruism

Of the two fables — the first illustrates voluntary altruism and the other illustrates involuntary (or forced) altruism.

---

3   A. Smith, *An Inquiry into the Nature and Causes of the Wealth of Nations* (London: Methuen, 1904).

4   F.Y. Edgeworth, *Mathematical Psychics: An Essay on the Application of Mathematics to the Moral Sciences* (London: C. Kegan Paul, 1881).

5   F.H. Knight, *Risk, Uncertainty, and Profit* (Boston: Houghton Mifflin, 1921).

6   The choice of these fables does not imply that I encourage these religious faiths. It is merely that these fables lend credence to my arguments that follow.

Voluntary Altruism. The Celebration of Onam in many parts of Southern India is a feast to welcome the spirit of King Mahabali who saved the earth by his ultimate act of altruism. The legend goes as follows. King Mahabali was a wise and generous ruler whose popularity and power were both steadily growing. This was irksome to an Asura King who recruited the help of Lord Vishnu to curb the growing power of Mahabali. Vishnu transformed himself into a dwarf named Vamana and arrived at King Mahabali's palace with a request for permission to build three steps to sit and pray. The generous King granted Vamana (Vishnu) permission. Vishnu who used his powers to become a dwarf now transformed himself into a huge giant and started building the steps. The first step covered the heavens and the second step covered the skies. King Mahabali realized that if the third step was built, it would cover and crush the entire earth. So, the kind and generous King offered his head as the third step so that the earth may be spared — an ultimate gesture of voluntary altruism. The earth is indeed saved and life goes on. Onam marks the day when the gods allow King Mahabali's spirit to mingle with his people.

Involuntary Altruism. Although I recollect this fable from a Church forum in the 1960s, I was able to locate its narrative through O'Shea (2001)[7]. The fable concerns the aspirations of three trees that get transformed into acts of altruism. These three trees had a conversation about their after-life, namely, how they would be transformed when felled. The first tree said: "I love babies — I want to be transformed into cradles where babies are rocked to sleep". The second tree said: "I want to see the whole world — I want to be transformed into a big ship that would sail across the vast oceans". The third tree said: "I want be left alone — I want to grow up and point the whole world to heaven". The foresters came with their tools. They chopped the first tree. Despite the tree's plea to be turned into cradles, it was turned into a manger for resting livestock and storing hay. It was in this manger that Baby Jesus was born. The foresters went to work on the second tree. To this tree's dismay they converted the tree not into a big ship but rather into an ordinary fishing boat. It was on this boat that Jesus stood on the shores of Galilee preaching his sermons to the masses. The foresters began chopping the third tree. The tree pleaded to be left alone to meet its aspiration

---

7   D. O'Shea, "The Resurrection", *Jacob's Well*, January 2001, downloaded from http://www. goodnews.ie/jacobswellvryheid.shtml.

of pointing the world to heaven. But it was chopped down and turned into a cross. On this cross, Christ was crucified. All three trees were forced to do something that they had not intended — but they ended up generating far greater benefits to humanity (at least from the Christian perspective) than they would have otherwise.

Both fables outlined above portray the greater good resulting from the pursuit of altruistic goals — forced or otherwise. Sustainability is explicit in the first fable. Moderation, a pre-requisite for sustainability, is conveyed in the second fable. A brief discussion of the sustainability principle is now in order.

Sustainability of Nature and Economics

A basic tenet in the economics of sustainability is that maintaining a steady stock of nature — otherwise referred to as environmental capital — is a necessary condition for economic sustainability. This is because nature plays a foundational role as both a *source* and a *sink* for the economy. It is a source for the basic resources the economy needs and a sink for the wastes which the economy generates. The depletion of the source and the filling up of the sink are invariably synonymous. Environmental capital is in fact a system of natural endowments that are connected through a complex network of bio-physical linkages without any geographic boundaries. Climate change is the result of the breakdown of these linkages. It is hence imperative that at least some bare minimum of environmental capital stock must be maintained in order to preserve our economic systems. This requirement is notwithstanding the need to conserve and expand the stock of natural endowments. Yet for many economists natural endowments are not essential. The following statement by Mankiw represents the beliefs of most economists:

> *Although natural resources can be important, they are not necessary for an economy to be highly productive in producing goods and services. Japan, for instance, is one of the richest countries in the world, despite having few natural resources. International Trade makes Japan's success possible. Japan imports many of the natural resources it needs, such as oil, and exports its manufactured goods to economies rich in natural resources*[8].

---

8   N.G. Mankiw, *Principles of Macroeconomics* (Mason, OH: Thomson South-Western, 2004), p. 246.

This is clearly a mistaken view on at least two grounds. First, natural resources are not simply extractable resources like oil. As indicated, they are a collection of linked endowments (including oil) that constitute ecosystems. Scientists now believe that it would be unwise to isolate ecosystems to local contexts given their global connectivity. That is, for example, when oil deposits are extracted in one location, the after-effects such as earthquakes can be felt elsewhere. Second, the potential to trade in extractable resources does not preclude the vital role of essential resources such as the air we breathe and the water we drink. In this context, then, the term *sustainable economic growth* is in fact an oxymoron. The economics of trade that Mankiw refers to fails to acknowledge the reality of global ecosystems. These misconceptions have their roots in the theory of perfect competition — where the sustainability principle is visibly absent.

Changing the Perfect Competition Benchmark

Consider first the inconsistency between the morals of the two fables and the theory of perfect competition as outlined in standard texts. Economists argue that the conditions of perfect competition represent a mere benchmark that enables the explanation of attaining the greater good. This greater good is in fact the maximization of net market benefits. Because markets represent the transactions across all members of society, market benefits are deemed synonymous with society's benefits.

The standard five conditions of perfect competition outlined in most texts are: *anonymity, homogeneity, perfect information, perfect mobility* and *full employment*. The *anonymity* condition dictates that every economic agent is a price-taker and will not be able to set price. The *homogeneity* condition implies that specific commodities cannot be differentiated by their producers (for example, by brand names). *Perfect information* ensures economic agents can replicate good practices and also make good choices. *Perfect mobility* indicates that desirable practices and goods and factors will enter without barriers whilst undesirable ones will exit. As the term suggests, *full employment* means that every resource is fully utilized.

When all of these conditions work together, the maximization of net benefits unfolds, and this represents the basis for explaining how a perfect market works in terms of what goods should be produced, how much of such goods would be produced, and how these goods could be produced. The formalization of the theory is to demonstrate the emergence of demand and supply and a unique market equilibrium price (P*) and quantity (Q*) at which the net benefit to society is maximized. Any deviation from the market equilibrium (P*, Q*) would result in a smaller net social benefit. Note that the larger the market, the larger the net benefit to society. Hence, formalization of the market and perfect competition also lends credence to an important axiomatic distinction between a *good* and a *bad*. That is, a *good* is one where *more is preferred to less* and a *bad* is where *less is preferred to more*.

Consider now the implications of adding a sixth condition — *sustainability* — and the benchmark could then be appropriately renamed Sustainable Perfect Competition. The greater good now would not merely be the market configurations that maximize net social benefits at present, but more importantly those configurations that maximize market net benefits indefinitely over an infinite time horizon[9]. In this context, then, the axiomatic definition of a *good* could be one where *less is preferred to more*.

Had the conditions of Sustainable Perfect Competition been the norm in economics, then the excesses in the markets which have been source of various crises would have been non-existent. Further, in line with the morals of the two fables, indulgent consumption and investment would have been replaced by modest and moderate economic behaviour. It would be pertinent for me to conclude with the words of one of my heroes, Kenneth Boulding (1945),[10] on the subject of excesses: *"Any discovery which renders consumption less necessary to the pursuit of living is as much an economic gain as a discovery which improves our skills of production."*

---

9   I have provided a formal treatment of this conclusion in my work. See J.D. Thampapillai, "Perfect Competition and Sustainability: A Brief Note", *International Journal of Social Economics*, vol. 37(5): 384–390, 2010; and J.D. Thampapillai and J. A. Sinden, *Environmental Economics: Concepts, Methods and Policies* (Melbourne: Oxford University Press, 2013).

10 Kenneth Boulding, "The Consumption Concept in Economic Theory," *American Economic Review*, 35(2):1–14, 1945.

33 Any Progress Towards Sustainable Development or at Least Sustained Development?

Cecilia TORTAJADA

My current research includes work on policy, governance, security, and strategic analysis of the environment, natural resources, and development-related issues from an interdisciplinary and intersectoral viewpoint. One of my research concerns is that of sustainable development, its failures and challenges, and its multi-level impacts on water resources. The following thoughts refer to this issue.

As population has grown, and as human needs have increased and expectations have changed, the natural environment that supports their growth has deteriorated, and the challenges faced by governments and societies have become more complex. In a race to promote the sort of economic growth that is able to sustain human development, inexplicably people themselves have been pushed from the centre of development debates and dialogues to the periphery: people have many times lost the irrefutable priority governments should have awarded them in the search for sustainable development.

Agendas promoting human development have become multifaceted. Priorities have focused on state and social institutions that advance equitable growth with widespread social, economic, and environmental benefits, economic infrastructure and provision of social services, enabling regulatory environments and policy instruments for public and private investments in priority areas for human development, and, more recently, technological mobility.

Over the years, effective governance has been recognized as an essential element for human development. It is regarded as necessary for the achievement of societal goals and increasingly emphasizes the importance of involving more voices, responsibilities, transparency, and accountability of formal and informal organizations. Effective governance in this sense is expected to be part of all decision-making processes, to embrace the relationships between governments and society, and to permeate laws, regulations, institutions, and formal and informal interactions.

In the quest for sustainable development, infrastructure has proved to be an indispensable component due to its role in reducing poverty and inequality and promoting economic growth. Good infrastructure is vital to help overcome growth constraints, respond to urbanization pressures, improve social and environmental conditions, encourage competitiveness and productivity, underpin improvements in the quality of life and social inclusion, and enlarge and speed up communication and mobility. This should make it a sustained priority for all public and private sectors but within a framework of sustainable development. Unfortunately, this is not necessarily happening. In many cases, infrastructural development seems to have become an end in itself instead of a means to an end, the end being sustainable development, with the human component at the heart of it.

As noted by Nobel Laureate Amartya Sen, the absence of infrastructure has a pervasive influence on poverty but at the same time is not a free-standing factor in lifting people out of it:

> It is one thing to understand that lack of infrastructure is often the principal causal influence on the genesis of poverty, it is quite another to see how attempts at deliberate and organized removal of handicaps of underdeveloped infrastructure may actually make a difference. Do public plans and programmes actually work (a natural scepticism given the shrill chorus we hear too often these days that "the best plan is no plan")? Can the differences that are made be seen immediately, or do they take an immensely long time?

This also seems to be frequently forgotten, not only by policymakers and politicians but also, surprisingly, by people who are not in desperate need of provision of basic services.

Prevailing wisdom suggests that infrastructure development should be based not on political priorities but rather on social and economic realities. Unfortunately, this is not always the case. Prevailing wisdom also suggests that growth and equity-promoting strategies should be used to assess what might be necessary for entire populations, but especially the poor, to access basic services, as opposed to deciding, after the infrastructure has been developed, how it could be used by the poor. However, this objective too seems to have been forgotten in the race for economic development. In reality and given the size and scale of infrastructure requirements, decisions do not occur without political interference — a fact of life even when many times monopolies arising from self-serving political considerations have resulted in reduced quantities and poor quality of infrastructure services.

It is widely acknowledged that one of the main challenges facing the world at present is to develop implementable policies that positively influence the lives of billions of people all over the world who live under very different situations. The profound implications for development caused by demographic changes, the severe strains on the environment that result from rapid economic growth, and the limitations that infrastructural deficits place on access to social services in many countries constitute the panorama marking the end of the Millennium Development Goals. The Millennium Development Goals in their totality are unlikely to be achieved. Was this due to poor planning? Was it that the complexity of development was not acknowledged from the beginning? Or was it that unachievable goals were selected to start with?

To add to this complexity, the relaxation of the one-child population policy in China has the potential to change the global dynamics of growth and development and may increase the already enormous pressure on human and natural environments. According to the 2012 revision of the official United Nations population estimates and projections, the world's population, 7.2 billion as of mid-2013, is projected to increase to 9.6 billion in 2050 and 10.9 billion by 2100. These calculations are based on projected fertility declines in countries where large families are still prevalent and slight increases in fertility in countries where, on average, there are less than two children per woman. With the new population policy in the most populous country in the world, the global situation has the potential to change significantly. This decision is likely to have immense implications in terms of environment, water, energy, and food securities, not only for China but also for the rest of the world, because it is from the rest of the world that China obtains the resources required to satisfy many of its needs.

As one can appreciate, achievement of the MDGs, ultimately aimed at reducing poverty and inequality, depends on numerous interrelated global issues as well as on many actors that can influence them through multiple pathways. Infrastructure that is properly planned, managed, operated, and maintained and which has the potential to deliver universal coverage is one of the critical elements for the achievement of these goals.

Now, there is broad evidence that infrastructure coverage and quality play a vital part in the economic growth of any country as well as in investments in human capital, with both direct and indirect effects in reducing poverty. Where are the national, regional, and global efforts to understand the actual impact on society not only qualitatively but also quantitatively that are based on data that is complete and reliable? So far, the situation is just the reverse, with policy decisions taken with data that is either inadequate, incomplete, or outdated.

Regarding water development, virtuous cycles, where growth and social policies reinforce each other, are still not in place, in spite of their importance for human development. In addition, the inability of national and local governments to meet their populations' basic water needs — many times because of poor infrastructure or lack of it, as well as poor operation and maintenance practices — has resulted not only in economic but also social and environmental costs all over the world.

There is an increasingly large and expensive agenda of policy actions and investments in infrastructure that need to be undertaken. The delay in doing so has resulted in growing numbers of people without access to clean water and the resulting deterioration in their quality of life from avoidable illnesses and premature mortality or morbidity, environmental pollution of point and non-point water sources, over-exploited and polluted rivers, lakes, and aquifers, depletion of non-renewable resources and higher costs of pumping groundwater, and seawater intrusion and land subsidence. These are just a few of the numerous issues that are affecting populations on a daily basis all over the world and that are, in many cases, already delaying social and economic progress, impacting negatively on livelihoods, degrading the environment, and hampering economic development.

For the provision of basic infrastructure services, such as water and sanitation, on which quality of livelihoods rely, and the infrastructure through which water is provided, long-term planning also leaves much to be desired. People's expectations and aspirations have changed significantly in recent years, requiring new policy responses and demanding participation, transparency, accountability, and responsibility, which was not the case before. This requires new multi-level governance practices that may or may not be possible or achievable.

To identify and understand these changes and to propose alternative policies, institutions, regulations, and strategies that are more relevant for the twenty-first century, it will be necessary to redirect policy dialogues to the fundamentals and to challenge the core of the development discourse. Development is about people, a fact that seems to have been forgotten in many places on numerous occasions. The earlier dominant role of policymakers in developing policies and trying to implement them in isolation has only a limited value in present-day society. Technocratic alternatives may not be compatible with reality until and unless societies and their views and expectations are made a part of development policy-making.

The above may be an explanation as to why, in the second decade of the 21st century, the formulation and implementation of efficient water quality management policy for the overall benefit of humankind and the environment has still not been achieved.

34 Making Research a Fulfilling Mission

VU Minh Khuong

Since childhood I have harboured a belief that we can improve on whatever we do by better understanding it. With abiding memories of war, hunger, and poverty, I never let a day pass without reflecting on how people can make their country and the world more peaceful and prosperous. Devotion to such causes is quite natural for me. It brings me not only satisfaction but also a sense of mission, not only joy but also fulfillment.

In the early days of my career, I passionately pursued this mission in my professional practice. In 1988, I was elected by more than 400 workers to be CEO of a chemical company located in Haiphong, my hometown. The company was on the verge of bankruptcy, and I will never forget seeing the emotional response of workers when I made and ultimately fulfilled my promise to revive the company. These memories further deepened my commitment to learn more about and engage more passionately in endeavours to create prosperity for the economically disadvantaged.

In 1993, right after the US had lifted its embargo against Vietnam, I was one of the first Vietnamese nationals to receive a Fulbright Scholarship, which enabled me to pursue an MBA at the Harvard Business School (HBS). At HBS, I first learned about Singapore's successful development story through a case study. The class fervently discussed the case, and many doubted the sincerity and feasibility of Singapore's ambition to catch up with the US on per capita income. Motivated by the Singapore story, I made my first visit to the country in 1994 on my way from the US to Vietnam. This visit deepened my resolve to learn more about how and why Singapore achieved such remarkable economic development.

I went back to Haiphong to serve as a senior government official after my graduation from the Harvard Business School. I made every effort in my limited capacity to transform the city with the Singapore model in mind. The opportunities at leading this transformation, however, were quite limited. I realized that I would be able to do more as an expert rather than as a government official. After five years of hard work and dedication with the government, I returned to Harvard in 2000 to pursue a PhD in public policy with a focus on economic development. I promised myself to learn as much as possible about economic development in order one day to come back to share my knowledge with my colleagues.

Influences

The academic paper that had the greatest influence on my research passion is "Making a Miracle," published by Nobel Laureate Robert E. Lucas in 1993.[1] The article aims to better understand the factors driving a nation's success. Its comparisons between the Philippines and South Korea in 1960 and their changes over the following 28 years were profoundly revealing. In 1960, when the two countries had similar levels of income, the conditions for rapid development were more favourable in the Philippines than in South Korea, particularly in education. The remarkable transformation of South Korea and other successful Asian countries within one generation, in contrast to the stagnation of the Philippines and other underperforming Asian countries over the same time period, can be regarded as an economic miracle. According to Lucas, "If we know what an economic miracle is, we ought to be able to make one." This declaration has shaped my research agenda since I was a PhD student at Harvard.

While articles and ideas can be personally influential, there is no more powerful force than a close and inspirational relationship with a trusted mentor. The person who has had the greatest effect on my research method philosophy is Professor

---

1   Robert E. Lucas, "Making a Miracle", *Econometrica*, Vol. 61 (2), March, 1993: 251–272.

Dale Jorgenson. I was very fortunate to have him as the primary adviser of my PhD thesis. His path-breaking contribution to the improvement of accounting methods has become the gold standard for productivity analysis.[2] His *growth decomposition method* provides powerful insights for policymakers to promote economic growth through structural change and information technology diffusion. I am proud to have co-authored with Professor Jorgenson a number of academic papers and plan to continue to do so in the years to come.

Motivation

The hallmark of my research is its powerful link between theory and practice. I entered into academics after having worked in the public sector for more than 15 years, holding positions with various levels of power. This rich experience has enabled me to deeply appreciate the importance of research that is rigorous but applicable to actual policy settings.

I have a deep passion to understand how policy measures transform countries from poor to prosperous, and this has been the main factor guiding my research focus and scholarly commitment throughout my academic career. The main areas of my research interests include economic growth and competitiveness, productivity, the impacts of information technology and globalization on economic growth, and Asian/ASEAN economic integration. These topics are not only growing in importance and complexity, but also receiving increasing coverage in the literature and providing the basis for an expanding network of regional and global research collaborations.

Insights, policy implications, and applications are the primary focus of my research, which is based on rigorous evidence-based analysis. I aim to help policymakers enhance their capacity and efficacy of decision-making by maximizing the visibility and accessibility of my research results. My research also targets scholars by situating findings within a broader theoretical context. I believe that applicability and theoretical novelty can complement one another, and my work has and will

---

2   Caselli Francesco, "Growth Accounting," in S. N. Durlauf and L. E. Blume, eds., *The New Palgrave Dictionary of Economics* (New York: Palgrave Macmillan, 2008).

continue to have broad interest among researchers and practitioners across public policy, development economics, and business.

Research plays a vital role in my career. It cultivates my passion, enhances my productivity, and reinforces my teaching effectiveness. My current and future research plans follow my passion to make meaningful contributions to better understand economic development in Asia and the policy approaches that developing countries must embrace to foster their catch-up endeavours.

My current and long-term research plans centre on the main areas of my primary research interests: economic growth, productivity, and competitiveness. With this focus, my research ranges from the impacts of ICT on economic development to the effects of Asia's rise on the world economy, the dynamics of Asian economic integration, and policy options for promoting economic development.

Research Plan

In the next five to ten years, my research will concentrate on the following three main programmes: ICT and development; the dynamics of Asian transformation and its impacts on the world economy; and policy options to induce productive behaviour.

ICT and development. ICT has immense potential to make individuals, companies, and nations more knowledgeable, effective, and collaborative. I believe that research about the impacts of the internet and mobile technologies can produce valuable policy insights to help people, businesses, and countries better exploit their capabilities, and to help the global community develop comprehensively, equitably, and sustainably.

The dynamics of Asian transformation and its impacts on the world economy. While Asia will likely experience unrelenting economic and geopolitical turbulence, it will also continue to transform at a remarkably rapid pace. The dynamics of this growth will be even more exciting, arguably as much for academia as for practice. For example, India's growth rate may surpass China's in the coming decades. Thoroughly understanding the dynamics of Asia's transformation and the factors underlying this process can provide important insights for companies and countries to better anticipate changes and more deftly adapt to reality.

Policy options to induce productive behaviour. Governments can solve many persistent problems with better policy options to enhance the productivity of people's behaviour. Traditional economics emphasizes the importance of cost-benefit analysis or stick-carrot approaches. In contrast, I am confident that beliefs, assumptions, and capabilities to foresee cost-benefits in the long-term play a more important role in inducing productive behaviour. This approach has allowed me and Boyd Fuller to publish a prize-wining paper about a policy framework to promote collaboration. I plan to further develop this approach to study other issues such as the control of corruption, improvements in the effectiveness of foreign aid, and even more complicated problems such as the Palestine–Israel conflict.

Research Passion and LKYSPP Future

An excellent school must continually reflect on its competitive position and brand image. What makes the world's best students choose LKYSPP? Low tuition and generous scholarships are not necessarily permanent or sustainable strategies, and location or diversity can make only marginal impacts on competitiveness. I believe that the wining factor in making LKYSPP distinctive is its faculty's research passion. This passion can not only enhance the global image of the school through impactful publications, but will also guarantee that faculty members are at the cutting edge of research and will demonstrate thought leadership not only in the academic field but also in the classroom. This can help prepare and motivate students to deal with real-world policy problems in their careers, thereby supporting the reputation of the school.

35 What Drives Public Managers in Tough Governance Settings?

Zeger van der WAL

Throughout my academic career I've been fascinated by the passion, drive, and abilities of all the senior civil servants I've met, taught, interviewed, and surveyed. Many of them operate in a minefield of conflicting interests and values, goal ambiguity, opportunistic political bosses, imperfect organizational structures, and ever increasing citizen demands. How do they manage to get anything done at all? How do they remain ethical and motivated to perform their duties with vigour and dedication while they could earn so much more with their skillset in a private sector setting? What makes them tick? And what are 'tipping points' that ultimately do lead to disillusion, burnout, and 'sector switching'?

These questions motivate and drive me in my own scholarly quest for answers and understanding of how some of these complex mechanisms work. In doing so, I combine insights and methodologies from Public Management, Political Science, Organizational Psychology, Management Studies, Business Administration, and Ethics. Interacting with our very own students — often rather seasoned public officials operating in what I would call "tough governance settings" — has further ignited my passion for this research subject. In fact, one of my key projects at the moment is a longitudinal study into values, work motivations, sector perceptions and career preferences of LKYSPP students in comparison with Business School students in which I also assess the impact of our degree programmes on the drivers and ambitions of these future leaders.

After I elaborate on this project and argue why I think it is so relevant in our current era, I formulate a position on the study of public service motivation (PSM) in tough governance settings and the (ir)relevance of current concepts of Western origin to conduct meaningful research in such settings. To conclude this essay, I will conclude with the outlines of my own research agenda to answer the key question in the title of this essay in the coming years as a faculty member of our great school.

What Drives Future Public Leaders? Studying our Own Students[1]

Studies into the values, motivations, and sector perceptions of pre-career students in public administration and business administration and senior managers in both sectors are without exception cross-sectional.[2] Longitudinal studies that consider both self-selection and socialization are almost non-existent.[3] In addition, empirical studies comparing the raw material — graduate students in degree programmes directed towards employment in one of both sectors are only beginning to emerge: Asia is a highly understudied region in this field.[4]

The lack of such studies prevents us from answering pressing questions that merit empirical consideration: Do different people types exist with a strong preference for an employer in either of the sectors based on different values, motivations,

---

1   Parts of this section are adapted from my Faculty Start up Grant submitted and approved in February 2013.

2   Redman-Simmons, L.M. (2008) Graduate Students' Attraction to Government Public Service Professions. Presented at *Minnowbrook 3 Conference*, September 2008, Lake Placid, New York; Van der Wal, Z., G. de Graaf & K. Lasthuizen (2008). What's Valued Most? A comparative empirical study on the differences and similarities between the organizational values of the public and private sector. *Public Administration* 86 (2): 465–482; Van der Wal, Zeger, and Anne Oosterbaan (2010). Bestuur of Bedrijf: Waar willen studenten werken en waarom? *Bestuurskunde* 19 (2): 58–69; Vandenabeele, W. (2008). Government Calling: Public Service Motivation as an Element in Selecting Government as an Employer of Choice. *Public Administration* 86 (4): 1089–1105.

3   Blau, Peter M. 1960. Orientation toward clients in a public welfare agency. *Administrative Science. Quarterly* 5:341–61; Kjeldsen, Anne-Mette, and Jacobsen, Christian B. 2012. Public Service Motivation and Employment Sector: Attraction or Socialization? *JPART*, first published online, October 29, 2012.

4   Infeld, D.L., Qi, G., Adams, W.C., Lin, A. (2009). Work Values and Career Choices of Public Administration and Public Policy Students in the U.S. and China. Presented at the *IPSM Conference*, June 6–8, Bloomington, Indiana.

and perceptions, prior to choosing their first job, or even prior to their choice for a particular educational environment? Do both sectors indeed cultivate and reinforce contrasts and mutual, cliché-type perceptions of sectors by replacing individual morals that do not match the organizational goals with an 'organizationally based collective ethic'? What about the hypothesis that any idealistic expectations held by individuals without work experience change after their employment, the so-called 'shock effect'? What *is* the exact effect of actual work experience on pre-entry career determinants and job preference? And, how about the impact of the degree programme itself? Even partial answers to these questions may provide important and innovative contributions, not only to public and private management theory, but also to human resource management (HRM) practices in both sectors, and even the design of degree curricula within public policy schools and business schools.

Answering this question is particularly relevant in an era in which distinctions between sectors might be less clear than ever before. Increasingly, high work pressure, businesslike management and organizational effectiveness are becoming characteristic of government organizations that also offer many good career opportunities with realistic rewards.[5] Concomitantly, many companies pay increasing attention to corporate social responsibility (CSR) and sustainability and thus to 'contributing to society' that students in public policy schools value so much.[6] Arguably, the factors which *traditionally attracted* different raw material are becoming *less and less distinctive*. Moreover, the newest generation that is about to join the employee ranks, Generation Y, is said to be motivated by doing good, making a difference, and serving public needs, *regardless* of which sector ultimately employs them, and to have a different attitude towards work values in general.[7]

---

5   Lyons, S.T., Duxbury, L.E. and Higgins, C.A. (2005). Is the Public Service Ethic in Decline? Paper presented at the *9th IRSPM Conference*, 6–8 April, Bocconi University, Milan, Italy.

6   Fortanier, F. and Kolk, A. (2007). On the Economic Dimensions of Corporate Social Responsibility: Exploring Fortune Global 250 Reports. *Business and Society* 46 (4): 457–478.

7   Holmes, L. (2012). Reaching Gen Y… Do you know how to speak to them? http://holmesmarketing. wordpress.com/2012/08/23/reaching-gen-y-do-you-know-how-to-speak-to-them/; Twenge, J.M. & S.M. Campbell (2012). Who are the Millennials? Empirical evidence for generational differences in work values, attitudes and personality. In: Ng. E., Lyons, S. & Schweitzer, L. (Eds.) *Managing the New Workforce. International perspectives on the millennial generation*. Cheltenham: Edward Elgar, pp. 1–19.

An intriguing question is if and how these developments have affected the degree programmes that are traditionally expected to produce students with distinctive value orientations, motivational profiles and sectoral preferences aimed at both sectors — public administration and public policy on the one hand and business administration on the other. These programmes have always had an institutional and financial interest in keeping alive the strong demarcations between both sectors. This might also explain why "all over the world public administration and business administration research and education are institutionally separated", except for the UK and parts of the US where public administration and public policy are sometimes taught within business schools.[8]

Thus, even though both degrees might still market for different types of students preferring different careers, the real-world convergence and blurring of sectors undoubtedly affected their curricula. Haven't public policy students in recent cohorts increasingly been taught that concepts such as "sector blurring", networked governance, social enterprise and public-private partnerships (PPPs) characterize the modern-day organizational landscape, and NPM-inspired businesslike government reforms have made strict sectoral demarcations less and less relevant? Much of the scholarly publications in business nowadays stress corporate social responsibility (CSR) and increasing public accountability obligations for the business sector. And what about the 'ethics pledge' MBA students have to take nowadays as a response to the endemic unethical conduct associated with the global financial crisis, suggesting that making money should not be their only, or even main, career motive? In short: one might say both content and context of public policy and business school curricula are not only *changing*, but also to a certain extent *converging*.

These developments have two important implications: one, if both characteristics and perceptions of sectors have become less distinctive we may wonder whether a choice for a MPP or MPA automatically leads to a career in government and the choice for a MBA to a working life in business. Two, we may expect the "raw material" that is about to enter the job market to be less different in terms of their values and motivations compared to two decades ago. Not only because of

---

8   Kickert, W.J.M. (1993) (ed.). *Veranderingen in Management en Organisatie bij de Rijksoverheid.* Alphen aan de Rijn: Samson.

the unique attitudes ascribed to Generation Y, but also because studies show junior public managers already differ from their more senior colleagues as they are driven by a good salary and career opportunities similar to their private sector counterparts, whereas (prospective) business managers increasingly believe firms have ethical, social, and even charitable obligations, stretching beyond the classical bottom line.[9]

However, what the cross-sectional data cannot show is whether *taking the programme as such* affected the motivations, values, and sector perceptions already held by the students. By comparing work motivations, personal values, sector perceptions and preference for future employer within one cohort at the start and at the end of their Master's programme, I want to *critically assess how our own teaching actually better prepares future public leaders* in terms of the drivers they will need to succeed in their complex operating environments, and to what extent it inculcates *the mission of our school. By comparing these characteristics just before graduation and 12–18 months after graduation* when our students have engaged in their first postgraduate employment experience *I want to observe how they may be affected by organizational socialization.* Both issues will greatly add to current knowledge of public and private sector managers and what it takes to build them.

Public Service Motivation (PSM) in "Tough Tovernance Settings"

One of the reasons for moving to Asia and LKYSPP in particular is my own curiosity to pursue my research passions in non-Western and developmental contexts. After all, in countries where not everything revolves around the upper echelons of Abraham Maslow's pyramid, being a government employee may have little to do with seeking intellectual challenges and self-fulfilment and more with survival, social status, and nepotism. All the more, questions concerning their motivations and how to incentivize better performance are of key importance in the pursuit of good governance but are not easily answered with instruments and concepts based on Western preconceptions.

In fact, one may wonder to what extent much of the current research into public service motivation (PSM) suffers from "aspirational bias" and perhaps even

---

9   Elias, R.Z. (2004). An Examination of Business Students' Perception of Corporate Social Responsibilities Before and After Bankruptcies. *Journal of Business Ethics* 52: 267–281.

"self-confirmation bias" as it employs — without much questioning over time — research instruments and assumptions rooted in the American ethos and folklore of "giving back to society", having "compassion" and "civic duty". Sparse studies using slightly different instruments or broader approaches to employee motivation immediately provide a different picture. For instance, a rare comparative study between MPP and MPA students from China and the US shows the former are far less driven by intrinsic factors.[10] Moreover, others argue that in countries such as China, India, Malaysia, Indonesia, Philippines, and Singapore, where government jobs have more societal stature[11] and often provide better primary and secondary benefits than private sector jobs[12], public and private sector employees may show different (and arguably less) contrasts than in most Western countries.

Unfortunately, only a handful of studies within the field have combined PSM measures with other motivational constructs, and they all show much more mixed results in terms of why individuals choose as well maintain public sector employment and less contrast between public and private sector employees than traditional PSM studies suggest.[13] More specifically, studies using multiple or longitudinal measures show that the motivational spectrum of public sector workers contains complex mixes of both intrinsic and extrinsic drivers, whose composition varies over time and when individuals move to more senior positions during their careers.[14] For instance, public managers are motivated by being close to power, enjoying good career prospects and conditions and even list coincidence when applying for jobs as

10 Infeld, D.L., Qi, G., Adams, W.C., Lin, A. (2009). Work Values and Career Choices of Public Administration and Public Policy Students in the U.S. and China. Presented at the *IPSM Conference*, June 6–8, Bloomington, Indiana.

11 Donna Lind Infeld, William C. Adams, Guanghua Qi & Nik Rosnah (2010). Career Values of Public Administration and Public Policy Students in China, Malaysia and the United States. *International Journal of Public Administration* 33: 800–815.

12 Taylor, J. & L. Beh (2013). The Impact of Pay-for-Performance Schemes on the Performance of Australian and Malaysian Government Employees. *Public Management Review* 15 (8): 1090–1115.

13 Buelens, M. and van den Broeck, H. (2007). An Analysis of Differences in Work Motivation between Public and Private Sector Organizations. *Public Administration Review* 67 (1): 65–74; Lyons, Duxbury, and Higgins (2005); Van der Wal, Z. (2013). Mandarins vs. Machiavellians? On Differences Between Work Motivations of Political and Administrative Elites. *Public Administration Review* 73 (5): 749–759.

14 Ritz, A., Brewer, G.A., and Neumann, O. (2013). Public Service Motivation: A Systematic Literature Review and Outlook. Revised version of conference draft. Prepared for the 2013 PMRA Conference, Madison-Wisconsin, USA, 20–22 June 2013. Under review by *Public Administration Review*; Van der Wal (2013). Mandarins vs. Machiavellians?

factors which led them to their initial or current jobs, whereas politicians (generally, a neglected population in motivational research) list factors such as ego and a strong belief in their own capacities to direct a policy or department in the right direction, or simply the fact that they were asked or "urged" to join public service.[15]

What I would argue our field needs to move forward and produce meaningful and relevant public management research for developing political economies is *a critical view on what motivates those operating in public sector environments in which pursuing the public interest sometimes is a mission impossible due to conflicting and ambiguous mandates and competing goals construed by corrupted or inert vested bureaucratic and political interests*. In addition, we need insights in what drives public managers (and how drives can be tweaked and affected by HR, reform, and performance related interventions) in settings where acquiring a public sector job simply is a means of survival, "disguised welfare", a favour by family or friends, or a widely sought after status symbol. Such public sector environments can be labelled "tough governance settings". It is highly questionable whether public sector work in such settings is all about "compassion" and "civic duty" and the like.

Gaining specific insight into what motivates both rank-and-file bureaucrats as well as administrative and political elites in tough governance settings is of invaluable importance to this field of study and may well elucidate why governance reforms and policy ambitions succeed and why they fail. In addition, *insights are paramount in specific organizational conditions and HR strategies* (whether intrinsic, extrinsic, or PSM-inspired) *that help to unleash "PSM vanguards"* and turn cynics and shirkers into well-performing change agents, and how PSM relates to ethical behaviour and willingness to change, among other things.

My Research Agenda in the Years to Come

It follows from all this that in contexts where public sector jobs are often more about survival and providing basic needs than about self-development and "advancing the public cause", public *service* motivation measures need to be supplemented with

---

15 Van der Wal (2013). Mandarins vs. Machiavellians?

public *sector* motivation measures and insights from Self-Determination Theory.[16] By exhibiting a healthy skepticism towards PSM while studying at the same time which mechanisms may stimulate and unleash intrinsic drivers within public sector workers in developing settings, we can acquire meaningful data. In turn, individual measures need to be supplemented with measures at the organizational level of supporting conditions for recruitment, retention, and development of motivated public sector workers.

Also, research in developmental contexts characterized by either insufficient or excessive levels of bureaucratic autonomy needs to take into account politicians as well, a neglected population in this area so far. Recent evidence on political-administrative dynamics from developing contexts that corroborate these dynamics are key in understanding any governance dimension and how it can be improved, including motivation.[17]

It is clear that there is enormous potential for studies that combine multiple measures over time and *relate shifts in motivations to HR and reform interventions and changes in the external environment of agencies* (economic growth, corruption scandals, etc.). Questions to answer in such follow-up studies include the following:

- How desirable is PSM at all in 'non-Western' or 'developing' contexts?
- *If* pursuing, nurturing and/or enlarging PSM is desirable, *how* can organizational support structures and HR strategies be devised that realize its potential in developing contexts?
- How can PSM be initiated, nurtured, and sustained in a context where (socio-economic) survival, job security, and vested interests of a career-based bureaucracy most likely dominate agency cultures and environments, and PSM has to 'compete' with other conflicting drivers?

---

16 Deci, E.L., Connell, J.P. & Ryan, R.M. (1989). Self-determination in a work organization. *Journal of Applied Psychology*, 74, 580–590; Deci, E.L., Koestner, R. & Ryan, R.M., (1999). A meta-analytic review of experiments examining the effects of extrinsic rewards on intrinsic motivation. *Psychological Bulletin*, 125, 627–668; Deci, E.L. & Ryan, R.M. (2000). The 'what' and 'why' of goal pursuits: Human needs and the self-determination of behavior. *Psychological Inquiry*, 11, 319–338.

17 See Development Leadership Program (DLP), http://dlprog.org/.

- How can PSM and related values be initiated, nurtured, and sustained through our teaching as public management and public policy professors?
- To what extent can existing approaches and strategies (mostly from developed contexts) be transferred?

I hope to answer some of these questions through my research endeavours in the region and beyond in the years to come, and by doing so, to contribute to the achievement of our school's mission: *Educate and inspire current and future generations of leaders to raise the standards of governance in Asia, improve the lives of its people and contribute to the transformation of the region.*

36 Dirty Boots and Polished Shoes

Robert J. WASSON

In my early teens I became interested in geology and, in retrospect, a desire to get out of suburban Sydney where I lived behind a shop. The only glimpse of 'nature' where I lived was a small patch of forest where I spent as much time as possible. I had started bushwalking and tried to make sense of the rocks that I saw and began collecting fossils. But I found myself interested in landforms more than rocks alone. My favourite landscape was the Blue Mountains west of Sydney, with its stark heaths on ridges, towering vertical cliffs of reds and browns that plunged into deep forested valleys. Although much of what he saw in Australia left Charles Darwin underwhelmed, the Blue Mountains captured his attention.

At the age of 16, I chanced upon a book by W.D. Thornbury entitled *Geomorphology* published in 1958. I was given it as a birthday present and decided that this topic was for me. At the University of Sydney, I studied geography, because it included geomorphology, and geology that at the time was resolutely focused just on rocks. I could not understand how the lecturers could tell us that highly deformed and metamorphosed rocks were formed during mountain building but took no interest in mountains as landforms.

More worrying was that geologists did not see geomorphology as a serious field of study let alone a science. So there was no rapport between scholars who now interact with good effect. I had encountered the first of many disciplinary disconnects. Geography also introduced me to the spatial functioning of human activities, sometimes within a historical context. Historical Geography still existed and the schism between physical and human geography was underway but not as profoundly as it is now. I was fascinated by landforms and so concentrated on geomorphology.

I found a field area 500km west of Sydney for my Honours research. On a sheep property, I investigated rocky hills that afforded a spectacular view of a vast and almost empty landscape, soils, sand dunes, rivers and lakes, all in an accessible and relatively small area. Just as at the age of 16 when I had an epiphany, the evidence of land and water degradation in my field area caused another shift in my consciousness. The beauty of the land simultaneously inspired me: most memorably as early morning fog lifted from the hills and valleys and lit up the stark white trunks of river red gums and the grey flanks of the high hills. The shapes and beauty of landforms captivated me, a sensibility that has remained with me.

I didn't realize it at the time, but there was a tension developing within me. At the top of my consciousness was a desire to understand the history and formative processes of landforms, but, in my sub-conscious, land and water degradation were becoming an interest. This interest burst out during a party with my fellow Honours students after we had submitted our theses and completed our exams, in my case in mathematical statistics. I lectured my friends that our environment was under threat, and we needed to do something. This was a time in Australia when the environment was the concern of very few people, the romance of the 'bush' was alive and well, and rural industries still counted for a substantial part of the country's wealth.

I wanted to study more but was uncertain where. So I took a job with the National Parks and Wildlife Service investigating land for conservation reserves, mainly in the arid and semi-arid parts of New South Wales. I was confronted by even more serious land and water degradation caused by overgrazing by domestic stock. I was horrified by the cavalier attitudes of some of the graziers. One night in a pub in the tiny town of Tibooburra I let the Friday night crowd of graziers know my feelings. A very large friend saved me from serious physical damage.

My dirty boots, so necessary for fieldwork, were replaced back in Sydney with polished shoes where I wrote reports that led to the creation of conservation reserves that have now recovered much of their former ecologic functions. But I decided that the intellectual environment of the bureaucracy was not for me, so I applied for PhD scholarships in the United Kingdom. This was the usual practice at the time for young aspiring Australian academics, and when I was offered a place I realized that we knew little of my own country, so why go elsewhere for a higher degree. I chose Macquarie University where there was a new vibrant School of Earth Sciences with academics from all over the world. I could get an international experience while studying my own landscape. By now I saw it as 'my' landscape, not the alien land that confronted the early Europeans who settled the country while displacing the indigenous people.

I taught undergraduates and studied landforms created by rivers and mass flows of mud and gravel, in Tasmania and Broken Hill in the desert. Once again land and water degradation could not be avoided, but I had a degree to complete and filed away my observations of degradation.

I was invited by geologists at Macquarie to join an expedition to the Hindu Kush in Pakistan once I had submitted my doctoral thesis, and so began my first experience of Asia. The route took us to Bangkok, Karachi, Peshawar, and Chitral where we camped for three months. I studied hillslope formative processes. I was overwhelmed by Pakistan, its landscapes and culture. Short visits to Quetta, Delhi, and Kathmandu sealed my fate. It was clear that Asia, and South Asia in particular, would be a large part of my future life.

I was still focused on basic research, so I studied landslides in New Zealand during a postdoctoral fellowship at the University of Auckland. Then a stint at Monash University back in Australia enabled me to begin research into desert dunes, one of the most regular of landform arrays on the planet. An opportunity presented itself at the Australian National University (ANU), then the hub of the most exciting work on arid Australia. I immersed myself in desert dunes and through the contacts of an Indian colleague spent six months studying the Thar Desert in India while based in Ahmedabad where I have lifelong friends and colleagues. But there it was again: severe land and water degradation in both countries.

That careers are often not planned but happen by chance was demonstrated by an unexpected opening at the Australian Commonwealth Scientific and Industrial

Research Organisation (CSIRO). My job was to discover how Australian landscapes had reached their parlous state since European settlement. I was ready. I could analyze the history and formative processes of landforms; land and water degradation had reached the top of my priorities; and I had begun to explore environmental history, enabling greater insights into the causes of degradation and how society has responded to degradation in the past and may in the future. I had found my niche, but now I had to work out how to assist natural resource managers and policymakers. It became clear that users of research need to be involved when research is first planned and that the right political environment is essential for research to hit its mark. Influencing the political environment is usually beyond the reach of researchers, but planning is not.

The set of skills that I had developed over fourteen years, with appropriate variations, was now applied to management of sedimentation in lakes, reservoirs, and swamps in many parts of the country, while meeting the requirements of the job. I also tackled problems of nutrient pollution, wind erosion, mine waste management and helped to develop sophisticated analytical techniques to quantify rates of change and sources of pollutants. I came to realize that, when problems are the focus, knowledge can be acquired from many disciplines. Making disciplines the focus is very limiting.

Polished shoes often replaced dirty boots, as I joined government advisory committees to assist policymakers in their craft. Politics usually took precedence over knowledge, sometimes because our advice would have placed livelihoods at risk. We were forced to understand that the environment could not always be the priority. Some of my colleagues, trained in environmental economics, began to explore how environmental repair could improve livelihoods. This message at the time was the most politically palatable but often difficult to demonstrate.

I also became aware of how environmental catastrophe pushes knowledge to the front, as in the case of a huge algal bloom in the Darling River. Politicians needed action, and we scrambled to give them what they wanted. This and other experiences suggested that we needed to keep generating and improving knowledge even if it was the minor partner in policy formulation because one day another catastrophe would occur, or motivated politicians and pressure from civil society would demand action and the knowledge would be needed. But short-term thinking began to take over from strategy, as governments demanded that our research should always have an immediate client.

The drive to turn CSIRO into a very expensive consultancy drove me to do what I had wanted for some time: return to a university. Now I used the management skills that I had learned in CSIRO, in various high level positions, back at ANU. Unlike many academics I enjoyed the challenge of helping teachers and researchers do their jobs better and to reach out to the broader community to let them know how their taxes were being used. I was also able to re-engage with Asia, something that I couldn't do in CSIRO. I returned to India where, this time, I focused on applied research on rivers, some of which has been used by Indians with policy influence.

The next step was to the Australian tropics where I took up the challenge of managing and expanding the research portfolio at Charles Darwin University. Here I was able to find time to work locally and in Indonesia, Timor Leste, China, Pakistan, and India, mostly with doctoral students. The most successful links that I established at this time were in northern Australia and Timor Leste, a young and extremely poor nation. Personal relationships formed the basis of collaboration with policymakers. Changes of government in both places reset our links and are still being rebuilt.

The same set of skills that I had now used for four decades was still relevant, but I was now confronted by two new challenges. The first was one that exercised my doctoral students. How can we justify research in a poor country using sophisticated techniques to which local researchers do not have access? The solution so far is to use a mixture of simple and sophisticated techniques. The simple techniques are available to local researchers, but partnerships will be needed between local agencies and research institutions for the demanding components. The second new challenge is how best to integrate local and modern scientific knowledge in a project servicing the needs of policymakers who have a modernist outlook? We keep trying.

By now the reader may wonder if I am bored with using the same research toolkit. The continuing relevance of my approach, using different combinations of its components, new challenges, and the diversity of policy environments has kept the passion alive. At the Lee Kuan Yew School of Public Policy I have an opportunity to: document much of what I have learned about the relationships between science, policy, and management; put the last three years of research at the National University of Singapore on flood histories and histories of human vulnerability to floods in a form of value to policymakers; and to work out why and how long-standing false policy narratives survive. I expect that polished shoes will be more common than dirty boots.

37 Warming up the Cold Bench

WU Xun

According to an old Chinese saying, "One's character at three years old seals his fate." When I was three years old, my grandpa made the prediction that I would be "sitting on cold bench" when I grow up. It is not difficult to image that my parents were not too impressed with the prediction, as I am the elder son in the family; but instead of contradicting my grandpa, they turned it into motivation for me: "Why don't you prove your grandpa wrong?!"

I asked my grandpa many times what he meant by "sitting on cold bench" before he passsed away in 1995, but I never got a definitive answer. He would explain to me that he believed I wouldn't be pursuing a career in the highly sought-after professions such as business or commerce and that most likely I would end up being a teacher just like my parents. My grandpa was a successful businessman in his heyday, and although such experiences took him to jail for over ten years after 1949 when the Community Party took over China, business and commerce had a special place in his heart all his life.

I set out to make my grandpa proud of me. After graduating from high school, I chose to study Business Management in an engineering university near my hometown, and four years later, I became a graduate student studying Business Administration in Renmin University in China. When I pointed out to my grandpa that I was pursing postgraduate studies in one of the most popular fields of study and in one of the best univeristies in China, he smiled but offered no correction to his prediction.

Maybe he knew better, as I have never been close to becoming a businessman. When I graduated from Renmin University, I was offered a position with the Instiute of Public Administration, a research institute established at Renmin University only a year before, and to the surprise of my classmates and even myself, I accepted the job offer. I still remember why I decided to take the job despite the low salary. The Founding Director of Institute, late Professor Huang Daqiang, made a pitch which I found irresistible: "Public administration is a new field of study in China, and you have the opprotunity to do something that has never been done before." Although I knew nothing about public administration or public policy at the time, this was all I needed to hear to make up my mind.

It was one of the best decisions that I've ever made in my life. In the Institute, I had the opportunity to contribute to the publication of the first book in China on policy science, a field of study to which I've devoted my career so far. I was asked to teach research methods in public administration which has since become one of my specialization areas. More important, it was in the Institute where I began my journey in search of better models to integrate theory and practice in public policy and governance.

The journey eventually led me to NUS where I secured a faculty position with the LKY School. I don't think that my grandpa would have been disappointed by the fact that I didn't end up in business. His prediction came at the height of the Cultural Revolution when I was three years old. Both my parents were sent to the countryside at that time to be "re-educated" by farmers because they held higher education degrees, and many universities across China were being closed down. My grandpa would have never imaged that it would be possible for me to be where I am today.

However, I have never forgotten my grandpa's prediction, and I believe that I've actually discovered some new meanings of the phrase "sitting on cold bench" in my long journey, trying to defy it. I think that it may serve as a useful reminder to me about the passion I have for what I do. The first is my passion for doing research in areas where limited work has been done, regardless of how familiar I am with the subject. The new areas may feel "cold", as much effort is required to warm them up. Such passion has driven me to venture into one new research area after another, such as transboundary water problems, urban water challenges, corruption, and research on public policy education.

The "cold bench", however, may not be the most comfortable place to be from time to time, and it demands persistence. I was drawn to doctoral training in public policy because it is a new field of study compared to more established fields such as economics, political science, and law, and there are a plenty of opportunities to work on 'greenfield' areas. However, my initial enthusiasm and commitment to "sit" on this "cold bench" were put under test numerous times during my years of doctoral study. I was uncertain about job prospects with this degree, and I seriously considered shifting to more popular fields of study such as economics, finance, and computer science, as most of my friends chose to do. Luckily, my passion has prevailed. Today, doctoral education in public policy has become one of the hottest degree programmes: we regularly get over 70 applicants annually for our PhD programme in public policy at the LKY School.

Another passion I have in research is to challenge conventional wisdoms. I believe that the persistence of policy failures in many policy sectors is due to the dominance of conventional wisdoms in policy thinking. The effort to demystify these conventional wisdoms may be regarded as "sitting on cold bench" given their dominance. My research work based on failures of health policy reform in Asian countries exposes flaws and inconsistencies in several guiding principles for health policy reform in Asia, and my work based on the study of conflicts in international rivers such as the Nile and the Ganges points to a surprising finding — that it is overestimation, rather than the lack of attention, which might be responsible for limited progress in conflict resolution in river basins.

Patience can be a crucial virtue when taking on conventional wisdoms. While there is tremendous pressure to produce research outputs as soon as possible in today's academic world, where one either "publishes or perishes," it requires substantial more effort and commitment to focus on debunking conventional wisdoms. For example, market failure is one of the most influential ideas in the public policy literature, but it has its share of limitations in the context of contemporary public policy challenges. My colleague M. Ramesh and I began our research on the deficiencies of the market failure perspective in 2006, but it took us almost six years to come up with an alternative framework after going through many iterations of our critiques as well as delving into new concepts.

The search for critical gaps that have been overlooked in the literature has provided a constant motivation for my research. These gaps are often "cold" simply because they have been neglected by other scholars. For example, studies of water privatization typically focused on external factors such as political support, institutional structures, the design of contracts, the transparency of the bidding process, and public perception and the impact of unforeseeable events, while little attention has been paid to internal factors. My research based on water privatization in Manila suggests that internal factors such as corporate governance, financial management, and operations management of privatized water utilities are among the most important internal factors that determine success in water privatization in developing countries.

Moving from one "cold bench" to another can be a risky strategy for a junior faculty member before he or she gets tenure. As an assistant professor starting my academic career in NUS, a piece of advice I often got from senior faculty members was that I should focus on a narrowly defined area for my research and publications so that I would be known in that particular area and that it can be risky to work on several different areas. But I find myself too weak to resist the temptation to work on the areas where I've discovered critical gaps, regardless of how they are related to my earlier work. Fortunately, I have not been penalized for pursing my passion, and I have been able to not only publish in top journals in all the areas that I have worked on, but have also built a stream of research in each of these areas.

I once asked my grandpa what he saw in me when I was three years old which convinced him about his prediction about my future career. He said that I was annoyingly persistent as a three-year-old and that I was surprisingly happy when left alone. Perhaps he was right after all about the "cold bench", and "warming up the cold bench" may best capture my passion for research.

38 Building an Asian Scholarship of Public Administration and Policy

Wai-Hang YEE

The rise of Asia has given scholars valuable opportunities to reexamine many of the established findings in the field of public administration and policy. With its distinctive historical and institutional context, Asia has much to offer to the intercultural dialogue. Ever since my graduate years, I have pursued this research agenda, focusing particularly on governing challenges related to the development of Asia.

My first major project examines China's environmental reform. Reforming China's environmental governance presents one of the most difficult policy and management challenges in the Asia Pacific region. During the past three decades of rapid economic growth, China has suffered from devastating environmental degradation. Yet lately the Chinese government has demonstrated increased commitment to fighting pollution and promoting environmental sustainability. Using mainly data collected from business enterprises with manufacturing operations in the Pearl River Delta, I seek to analyze the state-market interaction dynamics in the policy shift and hope to propose tailor-made policy solutions that can help sustain this important reform.

The other research project I am engaged in studies the governance of public agencies in various OECD countries. The worldwide administrative reform of New Public Management in the last two to three decades has resulted in a heterogeneous population of autonomous public sector organizations in many different countries. I have been collaborating with an international network of scholars, building together a cross-country dataset on these public sector organizations. In doing so, I seek to conduct comparative analyses in order to understand how the Asian political-institutional context influences this reform trend and shapes agency structures and performance.

The distinctive historical and institutional context of Asia, as mentioned earlier, plays an important role in my research. I believe that a thorough understanding of Asia's local institutions is crucial to resolving a lot of the policy and governance challenges in the region. Institutions are humanly devised and intersubjectively shared rules that govern our interactions. Rule of law, constitutions, various kinds of formal and informal decision-making, consensus-building and conflict-resolution mechanisms are all examples of institutions that can be commonly found in the action arena of politics and governance. Despite such commonality, conducting research on institutions has two main difficulties. First, institutions have many faces. One often needs to look beyond traditional disciplinary boundaries and conventional problem definitions in order to gain a comprehensive understanding of the nature and influence of institutions. Second, institutions are to human beings like water is to fish. Though their existence is fundamental to our society and sometimes our collective survival, they are very often forgotten or neglected. Thus in my empirical studies, I always try to trace carefully the influence of institutions. I seek to explore the impact of these underlying forces in multiple governance settings.

One analysis I conducted, for example, compared the reality of recent environmental governance reform in China against key arguments of ecological modernization theory, a theoretical model that generalizes Western European experiences of environmental reforms since the 1970s. My work found that although ecological concerns have gradually gained a foothold in China's existing political, economic, and to a lesser extent social institutions, the relevant actors and their patterns of interactions differ significantly from what the theory expects. In the institutional settings of China, local governments are assuming a more formalized relationship with firms in regulatory enforcement. Among market actors, organizational buyers along the supply chain have exerted more noticeable pressures on manufacturing firms than industrial associations and individual consumers. Civil society, while remaining less of an institutionalized actor in the environmental policy process, appears to pose a perceptible threat to at least some firms (Yee, Lo, and Tang, 2013).

Another analysis of the same project asks a rather different question — what drives regulatees' behaviours when the institution of law is weak? It came to similar conclusions. The analysis focused on examining the enforcement of environmental regulations in China. In the study, business enterprises were considered as regulatees, and they were interacting with environmental regulators from the local government. The results of my investigation were that the enterprises' decisions to adopt basic and proactive environmental management practices were less driven by concerns for legality than by their perceptions of the regulators' actions and gestures. Enterprises adopted basic environmental practices to avoid potential punishment and more proactive practices to avoid potentially arbitrary impositions from regulatory officials. Regulated enterprises were more likely to adopt both basic and proactive environmental practices if they had less difficulty in understanding the enforced regulations. These findings suggest important ways in which regulatory compliance behaviours in a developmental context may differ from those in Western countries (Yee, Tang, and Lo, 2014).

In analyzing the governance of public agencies, my colleagues and I also found that the influence of local governing institutions underlay our empirical results. One line of inquiry examined the extent and antecedents of management autonomies of government bodies in Hong Kong. In contrast with Western theoretical explanations of agency governance mechanisms, we found support for the thesis that administrative factors such as task and structure, rather than partisan politics which are common in democratic countries, serve as the key determinants in the executive-led government of Hong Kong (Painter and Yee, 2011).

In another study comparing patterns of agency governance in Hong Kong and Ireland in terms of their respective configurations of control and accountability mechanisms, my colleagues and I found that the elected government of Ireland's parliamentary democracy pays more attention to input controls, whereas the executive government of Hong Kong's administrative state favours output controls. Such a difference in forms of control and accountability reflect distinctive constitutional models of how political executives acquire and sustain their governing legitimacy. It supported our argument that how an executive government governs its agencies varies according to the constitutional setting in which it is embedded, with this relationship driven by consideration of the executive's governing legitimacy (MacCarthaigh, Painter, and Yee, 2014).

Recently, I have expanded the depth and scope of my quest for the hidden impact of Asia's local institutions. One major plan involves the collaboration with a research team based in the Civic Engagement Initiative at the University of Southern California, studying the social movement of homeowner associations (HOA) in China. This new neighbourhood-level institutional structure has much to offer to the development of a vibrant Chinese ethical citizenship and a better social foundation for the country's economic governance. In an initial analysis, my collaborators and I examined the relevance of traditional Confucian ethics to contemporary China. We argued that through HOAs a vibrant citizenship ethics may emerge from the Confucian tradition, helping smooth the interactions among local homeowners and solve various local property rights conflicts brought along by the maturing of the Chinese economy (Yee, Cooper and Wang, 2013). Further research is required to gauge the validity of these theoretical conjectures.

Another initiative builds on the existing work of my colleagues at the Asia Competitiveness Institute. With the help of a major national survey, we seek to investigate empirically the micro-foundation that links decentralization reforms and economic development in Indonesia. Specifically, we study how the quality of various governing institutions as perceived by business entrepreneurs mediates the effect of decentralization reforms in inducing their investment decisions (Yee, Li, and Amri, 2014). It is hoped that our analysis will generate important policy lessons for the implementation of decentralization reforms as well as the improvement of economic competitiveness in both Indonesia and other developing countries.

Without doubt many questions about institutions and how Asia's local institutions may shape the development of public administration and policy as a field of study are left unanswered. Yet as Ernest Hemingway once said, "it is good to have an end to journey toward, but it is the journey that matters, in the end". I am just glad that, in LKYSPP, I have the opportunity to work with many scholars of similar interests and commitments. I am sincerely grateful for that opportunity.

References

MacCarthaigh, M., M. Painter, and W. H. Yee (2014). Agency Governance in Its Constitutional Context: Comparing the Cases of Hong Kong and Ireland. Unpublished manuscript.

Painter, M., and W. H. Yee (2011). Task Matters: A Structural-instrumental Analysis of the Autonomy of Hong Kong Government Bodies. *American Review of Public Administration, 41*(4): 395-410.

Yee, W. H., T. L. Cooper, and W. Wang (2013). Ethical Citizenship and Collective Action: Chinese Homeowners' Participation in Neighbourhood Governance. Presented at the Public Management Research Conference, 20–22 Jun 2013, Wisconsin, United States.

Yee, W. H., H. Li, and M. Amri (2014). Decentralization, Governing Institutions, and Economic Development in Indonesia. Presented at the 2014 Asian Group of Public Administration Annual Conference, 27–29 Aug 2014, Jakarta, Indonesia.

Yee, W. H., C. W. H. Lo, and S. Y. Tang (2013). Assessing Ecological Modernization in China: Stakeholder Demands and Corporate Environmental Management Practices in Guangdong Province. *China Quarterly, 213* (March): 101–129.

Yee, W. H., S. Y. Tang, and C. W. H. Lo (2014). Regulatory Compliance When the Rule of Law is Weak: Evidence from China's Environmental Reform. *Journal of Public Administration Research and Theory*.

About the School

The Lee Kuan Yew School of Public Policy, National University of Singapore, was founded in 2004. Its mission is to "Educate and inspire current and future generations of leaders to raise the standards of governance in Asia, improve the lives of its people and contribute to the transformation of the region." It has sought to fulfil its mission through its teaching programmes, its research, and its outreach to the community as well as to international audiences and partners. Now in its tenth year, the School offers four Masters programmes and a doctoral programme, produces a broad range of high-quality research pertaining to Asia and global governance, and engages policymakers in Singapore and abroad. The School is home to four research centres — the Asia Competitiveness Institute, the Centre on Asia and Globalisation, the Institute of Policy Studies, and the Institute of Water Policy. It attracts students from Singapore, the rest of Asia, and the world, and its faculty come from Asia, Australia, Europe, and North America. As Asia rises, the School is committed to serving as a window into public policy and governance in the world's largest continent and as a gateway to global best practices.